Table of Content

A. Addressing the limitations of budget and equipment

B. Utilizing available resources to the fullest extent

C. Finding low-cost alternatives for equipment and editing software

4. Competition

A. Understanding the current landscape of the YouTube community

B. Differentiating oneself from the competition

C. Utilizing competition as motivation and learning opportunities

5. Time Management

A. Balancing YouTube content creation with other responsibilities

B. Creating a schedule and sticking to it

C. Delegating tasks and finding ways to maximize efficiency

6. Social Media Pressure

A. Understanding the pressure to be popular and gain followers

B. Developing a healthy relationship with social media and avoiding comparison

C. Focusing on meaningful and authentic engagement with followers

7. Privacy Concerns

A. Balancing privacy with the need to engage with followers

B. Protecting personal information online

C. Understanding the importance of online privacy and security

8. Feedback

A. Understanding the different types of feedback

B. Accepting feedback as constructive criticism and using it to improve

C. Dealing with negative feedback and avoiding online drama

9. Growing the Channel

A. Understanding the importance of consistency and persistence

B. Utilizing social media platforms and networking to reach a larger audience

Chapter 1

Introduction

YouTube has become one of the most popular platforms for creative expression and self-expression, especially for teenagers. With billions of active users and millions of channels, it's a place where young people can showcase their talents and reach a wide audience. But being a beginner teenager YouTuber can be a daunting task, filled with challenges that can make it difficult to grow your channel and reach your goals.

In this book, we aim to provide practical and actionable advice for beginner teenage YouTubers who are struggling to overcome the obstacles in their journey. We understand the emotional rollercoaster that comes with creating content and putting yourself out there for the world to see. The thrill of hitting that publish button and watching your views grow can be met with the crushing disappointment of low engagement and negative feedback.

However, we want to remind you that you are not alone. Many beginner teenage YouTubers face similar challenges and obstacles, and with the right tools and guidance, you can overcome them and grow your channel. This book is designed to provide you with the support and knowledge you need to succeed on YouTube.

One of the biggest struggles faced by beginner teenage YouTubers is the lack of content ideas. It can be frustrating to feel stuck and uninspired, wondering what topics to cover or what type of content to create. But with the right approach, you can overcome this challenge and find new and creative ways to express yourself.

Another common issue is the lack of resources. Whether it's limited equipment, budget, or time, it can be difficult to create high-quality content when you feel limited by your circumstances. But with the help of this book, you can learn how to maximize your resources and produce great content without breaking the bank.

The competition on YouTube can be fierce, with thousands of channels vying for attention and popularity. It can be easy to feel discouraged when you see other YouTubers with larger followings or more impressive equipment. But with the right mindset, you can turn this competition into a positive force that motivates you to grow and improve your channel.

Managing your time and finding a balance between YouTube and other responsibilities can be a challenge. It can be tempting to spend all your free time creating content, but it's important to find a healthy balance and avoid burnout. This book will teach you how to prioritize your time and find ways to be more efficient and productive.

Social media pressure can be a major concern for beginner teenage YouTubers. With the constant need to gain followers and be popular, it can be easy to get caught up in the comparison game. But with the guidance in this book, you can develop a healthy relationship with social media and avoid the pressures that come with it.

Privacy concerns are also a common issue for beginner teenage YouTubers. With the need to engage with followers and share personal information online, it can be difficult to protect your privacy and security. This book will teach you how to navigate these concerns and ensure that your personal information stays safe online.

Feedback is a crucial part of the YouTube journey, but it can also be a source of stress and anxiety. Whether it's positive or negative, feedback can shape your channel and influence your content. With the tips in this book, you can learn how to handle feedback and use it to grow and improve your channel.

Finally, growing your channel can be a slow and frustrating process, but with the right strategies and approach, you can reach your goals and build a thriving community. This book will provide you with the tools and advice you need to grow your channel and reach your target audience.

In conclusion, we want to remind you that starting a YouTube channel as a teenager can be a challenging and rewarding journey. With the right tools and support, you can overcome the obstacles and achieve your goals. This book is a guide to help you navigate the ups and downs of being a beginner teenage YouTuber. Whether you're struggling with lack of content ideas, limited resources, competition, time management, social media pressure, privacy concerns, feedback, or growing your channel, we've got you covered.

Our aim is to provide you with the knowledge, support, and practical advice you need to succeed on YouTube. We want to inspire you to be bold, creative, and authentic in your content and to help you grow your channel with confidence. Whether you're just starting out or you've been on the platform for a while, this book will provide you with the guidance you need to make your YouTube journey a success.

So, if you're ready to tackle the challenges of being a beginner teenage YouTuber, grab this book and let's get started!

Explanation of the Book's Purpose

As a beginner teenage YouTuber, you are about to embark on an incredible journey that is both exciting and challenging. The journey of content creation is not for the faint of heart, but it is one that is rewarding, fulfilling, and empowering. This book was written with the purpose of providing you with a roadmap to navigate the challenges that you will encounter on this journey.

The purpose of this book is to give you the tools and knowledge that you need to overcome the obstacles that you will face as a beginner teenage YouTuber. Whether you are struggling with a lack of content ideas, limited resources, intense competition, time management, social media pressure, privacy concerns, feedback, or growing your channel, this book has been created to provide you with a roadmap to success.

This book is not just another guide to YouTubing, but a personal story of triumph and success. It is written with a passionate voice and a deep understanding of the emotional rollercoaster that you are about to embark on. This book speaks to you in a language that is relatable, engaging, and full of emotion.

As a beginner, you are about to face challenges that can make or break your journey. The journey of content creation is not for everyone, but for those who are brave enough to pursue their passion, it can be life-changing. This book is written for those who are ready to take on the challenges and turn their dreams into reality.

For example, you may be struggling with a lack of content ideas. You feel like you have exhausted all of your creative energy, and you are unsure of how to come up with fresh and unique content that will engage your audience. This book will help you overcome your creative blocks and provide you with practical tips and techniques to find inspiration from sources that you never thought of. It will show you how to tap into your inner creativity and turn your passions into content that your audience will love.

Or perhaps you are feeling the intense pressure of competition. You look at other YouTubers with millions of followers and feel like you can never measure up. This book will help you understand that competition is a necessary part of the journey and that it can be used to your advantage. It will show you how to differentiate yourself from the competition, find your unique voice, and turn your channel into a source of inspiration and empowerment.

Or maybe you are feeling overwhelmed by the pressure of social media. You feel like you need to have the perfect life, perfect body, and perfect content to be successful. This book will help you understand that social media pressure is just an illusion, and that you can have a healthy relationship with it. It will show you how to focus on meaningful and authentic engagement with your followers and turn social media into a source of empowerment and joy.

In conclusion, the purpose of this book is to provide you with a roadmap to navigate the challenges of content creation as a beginner teenage YouTuber. It is written with a passionate voice and a deep understanding of the emotional journey that you are about to embark on. This book is not just another guide to YouTubing, but a personal story of triumph and success. Whether you are facing a lack of content ideas, limited resources, intense competition, time management, social media pressure, privacy concerns, feedback, or growing your channel, this book will help you turn your dreams into reality. So, let's get started on this incredible journey and turn your channel into a source of inspiration and empowerment.

Overview of the problems faced by beginner teenage YouTubers

Being a teenage YouTuber is an exciting and fulfilling experience, but it also comes with a range of challenges. For many beginners, the journey can be overwhelming, especially when they are faced with the following problems.

Lack of Content Ideas

One of the biggest obstacles for beginner teenage YouTubers is the lack of content ideas. The pressure to come up with fresh and unique content can be incredibly frustrating, especially when it seems like all the good ideas have already been taken. The fear of running out of content can leave many teenagers feeling creatively blocked and unable to move forward. However, the truth is that there are endless possibilities when it comes to content creation. The key is to find inspiration from sources beyond the YouTube world, such as books, music, art, and nature. By tapping into a diverse range of inspirations, teenage YouTubers can develop a content strategy that is both authentic and engaging.

Lack of Resources

Another common problem faced by beginner teenage YouTubers is the lack of resources. The equipment and software required to create high-quality content can be costly and, for many teenagers, out of reach. This can be particularly frustrating for those who are passionate about creating content but are limited by their budget and equipment. The good news is that there are many low-cost alternatives available, such as using natural lighting instead of expensive lights, or using a smartphone instead of a high-end camera. With a little creativity and resourcefulness, beginner teenage YouTubers can overcome these limitations and create content that is both high-quality and cost-effective.

Competition

The YouTube world is incredibly competitive, and this can be a major source of stress for beginner teenage YouTubers. With so many other channels vying for attention, it can be tempting to compare oneself to others and feel inadequate. However, competition can also be a source of motivation and inspiration. By focusing on creating content that is unique and meaningful, teenage YouTubers can differentiate themselves from the competition and carve out their own niche in the YouTube world.

Time Management

Balancing YouTube content creation with other responsibilities can be a major challenge for beginner teenage YouTubers. With school, homework, extracurricular activities, and social life, finding the time to create high-quality content can seem almost impossible. The key is to develop a time management strategy that works for each individual. This could mean setting aside specific times for content creation, delegating tasks, or finding ways to maximize efficiency. By taking a strategic approach to time management, beginner teenage YouTubers can stay organized and productive, and make the most of their time.

Social Media Pressure

The pressure to be popular and gain followers is a major issue for beginner teenage YouTubers. With so much focus on social media likes, comments, and followers, it can be tempting to compare oneself to others and feel inadequate. This can lead to feelings of anxiety and stress, and even cause damage to one's self-esteem. However, it is important to remember that the most meaningful and authentic engagement with followers comes from focusing on creating quality content, not chasing popularity. By building a healthy relationship with social media, beginner teenage YouTubers can avoid the pressures of comparison and focus on creating content that is meaningful and fulfilling.

Privacy Concerns

Another common problem faced by beginner teenage YouTubers is privacy concerns. With so much personal information being shared online, it is important to protect oneself from the potential risks associated with social media. This could mean limiting the amount of personal information shared, being careful about the types of content posted, and ensuring that online privacy and security measures are in place. By taking the necessary precautions, beginner teenage YouTubers can maintain their privacy and protect themselves from online threats.

Feedback

Receiving feedback can be both a blessing and a curse for beginner teenage YouTubers. While constructive criticism can help improve content, negative comments can be hurtful and discouraging. Dealing with feedback can be difficult, especially for those who are new to the YouTube world and are still developing their self-esteem. The key is to focus on the positive feedback and use it as motivation to improve, while also learning to ignore the negative comments that do not add value. By developing a thick skin and focusing on the positive, beginner teenage YouTubers can grow from feedback and become more confident in their content creation.

Growing the Channel

Finally, one of the biggest challenges for beginner teenage YouTubers is growing their channel. With so many channels vying for attention, it can be difficult to get noticed and attract new followers. However, there are many strategies that can help increase visibility and grow the channel. This could mean collaborating with other YouTubers, promoting content through social media, or leveraging SEO strategies to optimize content for search engines. With hard work, perseverance, and a strategic approach, beginner teenage YouTubers can grow their channel and reach their desired audience.

In conclusion, being a beginner teenage YouTuber is both exciting and challenging. From lack of content ideas to privacy concerns, the journey can be overwhelming. However, by focusing on the positives, developing a strategic approach, and tapping into a diverse range of inspirations, beginner teenage YouTubers can overcome these challenges and create content that is both meaningful and fulfilling. With hard work, perseverance, and a positive attitude, anything is possible.

Chapter 2

Lack of Content Ideas – The Biggest Hurdle for Beginner Teenage YouTubers

As a beginner teenage YouTuber, the thought of creating and sharing your own content on a platform watched by millions of people can be both exciting and intimidating. However, the excitement can quickly turn into frustration when you realize that coming up with new and interesting ideas for content is not as easy as it sounds. This struggle to come up with ideas can often lead to a feeling of defeat and discouragement, making it difficult for beginners to move forward with their channel.

In this section, we will explore the problem of lack of content ideas and provide tips and techniques to overcome this hurdle. By the end of this section, you will have a better understanding of how to overcome creative blocks and come up with unique and engaging content for your channel.

The Need for Fresh and Unique Content

One of the biggest challenges faced by beginner teenage YouTubers is the need for fresh and unique content. With millions of channels on YouTube, it's easy to feel overwhelmed by the competition and feel like everything has already been done. However, it's important to remember that the YouTube community is constantly evolving and looking for new and innovative content.

As a beginner, you have the opportunity to bring something new and different to the table. Your unique perspective, experiences, and passions can set you apart and make your content stand out from the crowd. By focusing on creating content that is fresh and unique, you will be able to connect with your audience and grow your channel.

Overcoming Creative Blocks

Despite the importance of fresh and unique content, it can still be challenging to come up with new ideas. When faced with a creative block, it's important to remember that this is a common problem faced by many artists and creators. Here are some tips and techniques to help overcome creative blocks:

Take a break: Sometimes, the best way to overcome a creative block is to step away from your work and engage in something completely different. Go for a walk, try a new hobby, or watch a movie.

Brainstorm with others: Collaborating with others can often lead to new and innovative ideas. Try brainstorming with friends, family, or other YouTubers to get fresh ideas and perspectives.

Try something new: Trying something new can often spark new ideas and inspiration. For example, try a new hobby, take a different route to work, or try a new type of cuisine.

Look for inspiration from other sources: Inspiration can come from anywhere. Try looking for inspiration from books, movies, or other YouTubers to get new ideas for your channel.

Finding Inspiration from Other YouTubers and Non-Related Sources

One of the best ways to come up with new ideas for content is to look for inspiration from other YouTubers and non-related sources. For example, you can:

Watch and learn from other YouTubers: Observe the style, editing, and content of other YouTubers to get new ideas for your own channel.

Look for inspiration from non-related sources: Inspiration can come from anywhere. Try looking for inspiration from books, movies, art, or even everyday life.

By incorporating these tips and techniques into your creative process, you will be able to overcome the problem of lack of content ideas and create fresh and unique content for your channel.

In conclusion, the struggle to come up with ideas for content is a common problem faced by many beginner teenage YouTubers. However, by focusing on creating fresh and unique content, overcoming creative blocks,and seeking inspiration from other sources, you can overcome this hurdle and succeed in your journey as a YouTuber. Remember, creativity is not something that comes overnight. It takes time, practice, and patience to develop. So don't be discouraged if you don't have the perfect idea right away. Keep experimenting and trying new things until you find what works for you. The important thing is to never give up and continue to chase your dreams and passions. With hard work and determination, you can overcome the lack of content ideas and create a successful channel that you can be proud of.

Understanding the importance of fresh and unique content

As a beginner teenage YouTuber, creating fresh and unique content is essential to your success. In today's world, there is an abundance of information readily available at our fingertips. With so much content available, it's important to stand out and create something that is both fresh and unique. The importance of original content can be described as the difference between standing out in a crowded room or blending in with the rest. Your content is the foundation of your channel, and without it, your channel will fail to grow and flourish.

Creating fresh and unique content is not just about differentiating yourself from others, it also shows that you are dedicated and passionate about your channel. It's a way of saying to your audience, "I am here to provide you with something that no one else can offer." This type of content creates an emotional connection with your audience, and when they feel a connection, they are more likely to engage with your content, share it with others, and subscribe to your channel.

The process of creating fresh and unique content can be a daunting task, but it doesn't have to be. With the right approach and a bit of creativity, you can develop content that will have your audience eager to tune in every time you post. Here are a few examples of fresh and unique content that you can incorporate into your channel:

Behind the Scenes: Share your life with your audience. Give them a glimpse into what goes on behind the scenes of your channel. This type of content is relatable, and it helps your audience connect with you on a personal level.

Collaborations: Collaborate with other YouTubers or content creators in your niche. This not only provides new content for your audience, but it also helps you expand your network and reach a new audience.

Vlogs: Vlogs are a great way to showcase your personality and connect with your audience. Share your day-to-day life, your thoughts, and your experiences. This type of content is personal and intimate, and it helps your audience feel like they are a part of your life.

Tutorials: Teach your audience something new. Whether it's a tutorial on how to do something or a lesson on a subject you're knowledgeable about, this type of content is both informative and engaging.

Q&A: Respond to your audience's questions in a video format. This type of content not only provides valuable information, but it also helps you connect with your audience and build a sense of community.

In conclusion, creating fresh and unique content is crucial to the success of your channel. It sets you apart from others, creates an emotional connection with your audience, and provides value to your viewers. With a bit of creativity, you can develop content that will have your audience eager to tune in every time you post. Remember, your content is the foundation of your channel, and with fresh and unique content, you can lay a solid foundation that will help you grow and flourish.

Overcoming Creative Blocks and Brainstorming Techniques

As a teenage YouTuber, you're faced with the challenge of constantly coming up with fresh, exciting content for your viewers. But sometimes, no matter how hard you try, you can't seem to think of anything new and creative. This is what's known as a creative block, and it's a common obstacle that every creative person faces at some point in their journey.

However, creative blocks don't have to hold you back from producing amazing content for your channel. With the right tools and techniques, you can overcome these roadblocks and tap into your full potential. In this section, we'll take a look at some effective ways to overcome creative blocks and brainstorm new ideas for your content.

Understand Your Creative Process

The first step in overcoming creative blocks is to understand your own creative process. Everyone's process is different, so it's important to know what works best for you. Some people are more creative in the morning, while others find inspiration in the evening. Some people need complete silence to create, while others work best with music or other background noise. Understanding your own creative process can help you identify what's holding you back and find the right solutions to overcome it.

Change Your Environment

Sometimes, all it takes to overcome a creative block is to change your environment. This could mean moving to a different room, going for a walk, or simply changing your posture. By breaking your routine and changing your surroundings, you can stimulate your mind and get the creative juices flowing again.

Take a Break

If you've been working on a project for hours and are still feeling stuck, it might be time to take a break. Going for a walk, listening to music, or doing something completely unrelated to your project can help you clear your mind and come back with fresh perspectives.

Collaborate with Others

Working with others can be an effective way to overcome creative blocks and generate new ideas. By bouncing ideas off each other, you can spark new insights and perspectives that you might not have thought of on your own. Collaborating with other YouTubers or even friends and family can also be a great way to network and gain new followers.

Use Mind Maps

Mind maps are a great tool for overcoming creative blocks and brainstorming new ideas. By creating a visual representation of your ideas, you can see the connections between them and find new ways to build upon them. Mind maps can also help you organize your thoughts and see your ideas in a new light.

Get Inspired by Others

Another way to overcome creative blocks is to get inspired by others. This could mean watching other YouTubers, reading books, or even looking at artwork or photographs. Seeing how others have tackled similar challenges can help you come up with new ideas and perspectives for your own content.

Keep a Journal

Keeping a journal is a great way to record your thoughts, ideas, and inspiration. By writing down your ideas as they come to you, you can prevent them from slipping away and keep track of what you've already tried. You can also use your journal as a reference when you need a fresh idea for your next video.

Don't Be Afraid to Experiment

Finally, don't be afraid to experiment and try new things. Whether it's a new editing style, a new type of content, or a new format for your videos, experimenting can help you break out of your comfort zone and find new inspiration.

In conclusion, overcoming creative blocks is a challenge that every YouTuber faces at some point in their journey. However, with the right tools and techniques, you can overcome these obstacles and tap into your full potential. Whether it's changing your environment, taking a break, collaborating with others, using mind maps, getting inspired by others, keeping a journal, or experimenting, there are many ways to overcome creative blocks and generate new ideas for your content.

The key is to find what works best for you and stick with it. Everyone's creative process is different, so don't be afraid to experiment and find what works best for you. Remember, creativity is not a finite resource, it's a muscle that can be exercised and strengthened over time. With practice and perseverance, you can overcome any creative block and produce amazing content for your channel.

So, the next time you're feeling stuck and can't seem to come up with new ideas, take a step back and try one of these techniques. You might be surprised by the new perspectives and inspiration that you'll find. And most importantly, never give up. The journey to becoming a successful YouTuber is a long and challenging one, but with hard work and dedication, anything is possible.

Finding inspiration from other YouTubers and non-related sources

Finding inspiration is essential for creating content that is fresh, unique and engaging. For beginner teenage YouTubers, the task of coming up with new ideas can be overwhelming, especially when surrounded by a sea of talented and experienced content creators. However, it's important to remember that inspiration can come from unexpected sources, including other YouTubers and non-related sources.

Inspiring and learning from other YouTubers can help jumpstart your creativity. From the way they structure their videos, to the topics they cover, there's a lot to be learned from watching and analyzing other content creators. For example, you can take inspiration from the way a YouTuber handles their transitions, incorporates humor, or incorporates interactive elements in their videos. You can also look at their niche and see how they are catering to their audience. By studying their successes and learning from their mistakes, you can develop your own unique style that appeals to your followers.

Non-related sources, on the other hand, can offer a whole new perspective and bring fresh ideas to the table. For example, if you are a beauty YouTuber, you can look to fashion blogs and magazines for inspiration, or if you are a gamer, you can take inspiration from the latest movies and TV shows. This can help you create content that is relevant and up-to-date, making it more likely to be noticed by your followers and draw new viewers to your channel.

Moreover, exploring different interests and hobbies can also spark new ideas. For instance, if you are an avid reader, try incorporating book reviews into your content, or if you love photography, share your experiences and tips with your followers. By incorporating your passions and interests into your content, you will not only be sharing a part of yourself with your followers but also providing a unique angle that sets you apart from others.

It's also worth exploring your local area, as you may find inspiration in the things around you. Whether it's a local festival, an event, or even your own neighborhood, there's a wealth of content to be found right on your doorstep. For example, if you live in a city, document your experiences of the vibrant culture, food, and people. If you live in a rural area, showcase the beauty of nature and the serenity of your surroundings. By doing so, you can offer your followers a fresh and unique perspective that they may not have seen before.

At the end of the day, it's essential to remember that inspiration can come from anywhere and at any time. Whether it's from other YouTubers, non-related sources or even personal experiences, be open to new ideas and never stop exploring. The key is to find what inspires you, and then channel that inspiration into your content. With each video, you will find that your creativity will grow, and you will be able to create content that not only sets you apart from others but also resonates with your followers.

In conclusion, finding inspiration from other YouTubers and non-related sources can help beginner teenage YouTubers overcome their creative blocks and create content that is fresh and unique. By exploring different interests and hobbies, incorporating personal experiences, and learning from other content creators, you can develop your own style and stand out in a crowded and competitive landscape. So, don't be afraid to step outside of your comfort zone, embrace new ideas, and never stop exploring. The possibilities are endless, and the rewards are immeasurable.

Chapter 3

Lack of Resources: The Constant Struggle for Beginner Teenage YouTubers

As a beginner teenage YouTuber, you are filled with excitement, passion, and creativity. You have ideas for videos that you know will captivate your audience, but there is one major obstacle standing in your way: lack of resources. This can be a heartbreaking and disheartening reality, but it is something that many beginner YouTubers face.

Starting a YouTube channel can be an expensive venture. You need equipment, editing software, and other resources to create high-quality content. When you don't have the money to invest in these things, it can feel like your dreams are slipping away. You may even feel defeated before you've even had a chance to start. The frustration and disappointment are palpable, and it can be easy to feel like giving up.

But it's important to remember that you don't need the latest and greatest equipment to be successful on YouTube. There are plenty of ways to overcome the limitations of budget and resources. You just need to be creative and resourceful.

For example, instead of buying expensive cameras and lighting equipment, try using your smartphone or a simple digital camera. Many smartphones now have great cameras and are more than capable of capturing high-quality footage. Invest in a tripod or stabilizer to keep your shots steady and professional looking.

If you're struggling with editing software, there are plenty of free or low-cost options available. iMovie is a great choice for Mac users, and Windows Movie Maker is a simple, yet effective option for PC users. These programs offer many of the same features as the more expensive software, and they are more than enough for most beginner YouTubers.

Another way to overcome the limitations of budget and resources is to be resourceful. Find ways to repurpose items you already have in your home. For example, use a cardboard box to create a DIY green screen or use a piece of cloth as a backdrop. These simple solutions can have a big impact on the quality of your videos.

It's also important to remember that you don't have to do everything yourself. Consider teaming up with other beginner YouTubers in your area to pool resources and share ideas. This can be a great way to get more equipment and create more diverse content.

While it can be frustrating to face the limitations of budget and resources, it's important to remember that these limitations can also be a blessing in disguise. They force you to be creative, resourceful, and innovative. These are skills that will serve you well in any area of your life, not just on YouTube.

In conclusion, lack of resources can be a major obstacle for beginner teenage YouTubers, but it doesn't have to be. By being creative, resourceful, and innovative, you can overcome these limitations and create high-quality content that your audience will love. Don't let the limitations of budget and resources hold you back from achieving your dreams. Embrace the challenge and make the most of what you have. The only limit is your imagination.

Addressing the limitations of budget and equipment

As a beginner teenager YouTuber, the idea of creating high-quality content may seem daunting. One of the biggest challenges you may face is the limitations of budget and equipment. The thought of not having the latest camera or editing software can be discouraging and make you feel like you can't compete with the big names in the industry. But the truth is, you don't need a massive budget or the latest gear to create amazing content. You just need to get creative and find ways to maximize the resources you have.

Imagine feeling empowered and confident in your content creation, knowing that you have overcome the limitations of budget and equipment. That is possible, and this section will show you how.

The first step to overcoming the limitations of budget and equipment is to understand that your content is not defined by the gear you use. It's all about the story you're telling and the message you're trying to convey. The audience will connect with your content if it's genuine, entertaining, or informative, not because of the equipment used. In fact, some of the biggest YouTubers started with just a smartphone and a simple editing app.

So, how can you make the most of what you have? One way is to utilize natural lighting to your advantage. Light is an essential element of any video, and you can make use of natural light to create stunning visuals without having to invest in expensive lighting equipment. You can also experiment with different angles and camera movements to add depth and interest to your shots.

Another way to overcome the limitations of budget and equipment is to utilize free editing software. While paid software like Adobe Premiere Pro or Final Cut Pro is great, there are also many free options available that offer similar features. iMovie, Lightworks, and HitFilm Express are just a few of the free editing software options that you can use to create professional-looking videos.

In addition to editing software, you can also utilize free or low-cost stock footage and sound effects to enhance your videos. Websites like Pexels and Unsplash offer free stock footage and photos, while websites like AudioJungle and AudioBlocks offer royalty-free sound effects and music. These resources can add an extra layer of production value to your videos, making them stand out and engage your audience even more.

Finally, consider collaborating with other YouTubers. Not only is this a great way to network and build relationships, but it can also help you overcome the limitations of budget and equipment. By working with others, you can pool your resources and create content that you may not have been able to create on your own.

In conclusion, the limitations of budget and equipment should not stop you from pursuing your passion as a beginner teenager YouTuber. With a bit of creativity and resourcefulness, you can overcome these challenges and create high-quality content that resonates with your audience. So don't let budget and equipment hold you back. Embrace the limitations and make the most of what you have. The sky's the limit!

Utilizing available resources to the fullest extent

As a beginner teenage YouTuber, it can be discouraging to feel limited by your resources. Whether it be a small budget, limited equipment, or limited editing software, these limitations can hold you back from reaching your full potential. However, it's important to remember that even the most successful YouTubers started with limited resources. The key is to utilize what you have to the fullest extent possible.

Imagine the excitement and sense of accomplishment you will feel when you create high-quality content that captures your vision, despite having limited resources. It's a feeling that is truly empowering and can propel you forward in your journey as a YouTuber.

One of the best ways to utilize your resources is to think creatively and find low-cost alternatives for equipment and editing software. For example, instead of investing in a high-end camera, you can use your smartphone camera to record videos. There are many editing apps available for smartphones that are free or have low-cost subscriptions.

Additionally, you can utilize natural lighting in your environment instead of investing in expensive lighting equipment. Experiment with different times of the day and locations to find the best lighting for your videos. Utilizing natural light can also help create a more authentic and personal feel to your videos.

Another way to maximize your resources is to delegate tasks and find ways to maximize your efficiency. This can include partnering with other YouTubers to collaborate on videos, delegating editing tasks to friends and family members, or finding interns or volunteers to help with filming and editing. By working together, you can divide the workload and utilize each other's strengths to create high-quality content.

Furthermore, you can use free online tools to help with your editing and marketing efforts. There are many websites and apps available that offer free music and sound effects for your videos, or even help you create eye-catching graphics and animations. Utilizing these resources can help you create professional-looking videos without breaking the bank.

Lastly, it's important to remember that content is king. The quality of your content is what will set you apart from the competition and attract viewers. Instead of focusing on expensive equipment and editing software, focus on developing your content and your unique voice. Be creative, be authentic, and let your passion shine through in your videos.

In conclusion, by utilizing available resources to the fullest extent, you can overcome the limitations of a small budget, limited equipment, and limited editing software. With a bit of creativity and hard work, you can create high-quality videos that capture your vision and reach a larger audience. Remember, the key is to never let limitations hold you back and to always focus on developing quality content that resonates with your viewers. So unleash your creativity, let your passion shine, and utilize your resources to reach your full potential as a beginner teenage YouTuber!

Finding low-cost alternatives for equipment and editing software

Finding low-cost alternatives for equipment and editing software is a common problem faced by beginner teenage YouTubers. With limited budgets, it can be difficult to create high-quality content and compete with others in the YouTube community. However, this should not discourage you from pursuing your passion. The truth is, you don't need expensive equipment or editing software to make great content. With a little creativity and effort, you can create videos that will captivate your audience and help you stand out from the crowd.

The first step in finding low-cost alternatives is to understand the equipment you actually need. For example, you don't need a professional-grade camera to start creating content. Your smartphone can easily serve as your camera, especially if you're just starting out. With the advancements in smartphone cameras, you can take high-quality videos and photos that will look great on YouTube.

Next, when it comes to editing software, there are many affordable and even free options available. Adobe Premiere Pro and Final Cut Pro X are two popular editing software options, but they can be costly, especially for beginners. Alternatives like Lightworks, Blender, and iMovie are all free to use and offer powerful editing capabilities, making them a great option for those who are just starting out.

However, it's important to note that finding low-cost alternatives for equipment and editing software is not just about saving money. It's about creativity, flexibility, and having the ability to make the most of what you have. For example, if you don't have a professional lighting setup, try shooting your videos outside on a sunny day or use natural light from windows in your home. If you don't have a fancy camera, try using your smartphone and experiment with different angles, shots, and lighting to see what works best for you.

The goal is to make your content stand out, not just through expensive equipment, but through creativity and originality. Embrace the limitations of your resources and use them to your advantage. For example, if you're creating a cooking channel, focus on the simplicity and affordability of the ingredients you use, rather than the equipment.

In conclusion, finding low-cost alternatives for equipment and editing software is not only about saving money, but it's also about creativity and originality. Don't let limited resources stop you from pursuing your passion on YouTube. With a little effort and creativity, you can make great content that will captivate your audience and help you stand out from the crowd. So, don't let the fear of high costs hold you back, embrace the limitations of your resources, and let your creativity soar!

Chapter 4

Competition

Competition is a natural part of life, and the YouTube world is no exception. In the online community, it can be overwhelming to see so many other talented and creative individuals sharing their content and building their audiences. The competitive environment can bring both excitement and stress to beginner teenage YouTubers.

For some, competition is a source of inspiration and motivation. It pushes them to create better content, improve their skills, and grow their channel. However, for others, it can be a source of anxiety and stress. The pressure to constantly outperform others and gain more followers can be overwhelming, leading to burnout and a loss of passion for the platform.

The key to navigating the competitive landscape of YouTube is finding a healthy balance. On one hand, competition can be a valuable tool for growth and improvement. For example, watching other

YouTubers in your niche can provide inspiration for new ideas and give you a better understanding of the types of content your audience enjoys. On the other hand, it's important to avoid getting caught up in the numbers game and comparing yourself to others.

One of the biggest challenges for beginner teenage YouTubers is to differentiate themselves from the competition. With so many creators out there, it can be difficult to stand out and find your unique voice. The temptation to imitate others or conform to what is popular is strong, but it is essential to maintain authenticity and remain true to yourself. This is what will make your content stand out and attract loyal followers who appreciate your individuality.

For example, one teenage YouTuber who found success by staying true to herself is Zoella. She began her channel sharing makeup tutorials and fashion tips, but she quickly gained recognition for her relatable and authentic personality. Zoella's fans appreciate her down-to-earth demeanor and her ability to connect with her audience in a real and meaningful way.

Another way to use competition to your advantage is to learn from your competitors. Observing their strengths and weaknesses can help you improve your own content and build a stronger channel. However, it's crucial to avoid copying or stealing ideas. Instead, use the information you gather to develop your own unique approach and style.

It's important to remember that competition is not just about outperforming others, it's also about improving yourself. The pressure to constantly produce new and exciting content can be overwhelming, but it's essential to take care of yourself and maintain a healthy work-life balance.

In conclusion, competition can be both a blessing and a curse for beginner teenage YouTubers. The key is to find a healthy balance and use competition to your advantage. Remember to stay true to yourself, differentiate from the competition, learn from your competitors, and take care of yourself. With these tips, you can harness the power of competition to grow your channel and achieve your goals.

Understanding the current landscape of the YouTube community

Understanding the current landscape of the YouTube community is a crucial step for beginner teenage YouTubers on their journey to success. The YouTube community is constantly evolving and changing, making it challenging to keep up with the latest trends and best practices. In this fast-paced and highly competitive world, it's essential to understand what sets your channel apart from the millions of others on the platform.

As you dive into the YouTube community, you'll quickly realize that the competition is fierce. With millions of active users, it can be easy to feel overwhelmed and discouraged. But, don't let that stop you from pursuing your passion. The current landscape of the YouTube community is filled with endless opportunities and endless creativity, waiting to be explored.

One of the most notable aspects of the current landscape is the sheer diversity of content. From vlogs and unboxings, to tutorials and comedy skits, there is something for everyone on YouTube. This diversity of content is what makes YouTube such a special platform, but it also means that competition is fierce. To stand out, you need to find your niche and make it your own.

One way to differentiate yourself from the competition is to bring a unique perspective to your content. For example, if you're interested in cooking, don't just focus on recipes and cooking techniques. Instead, consider incorporating your own experiences and cultural background into your content. This will make your channel stand out and give your audience a fresh and exciting take on cooking.

Another way to set your channel apart is to bring a level of authenticity to your content. With so much content available on YouTube, audiences are looking for something real and relatable. They want to connect with the person behind the camera and feel a sense of genuine connection. So, be yourself, and don't be afraid to show your personality and let your audience get to know the real you.

In addition to the diversity of content, the YouTube community is also known for its tight-knit community. The platform provides a space for YouTubers to connect, collaborate, and support each other. This supportive community is a valuable resource for beginner YouTubers. It provides a sense of belonging, as well as a source of inspiration and motivation.

One example of this tight-knit community is the number of collaborations and cross-promotions that happen on YouTube. By working together, YouTubers can reach a larger audience and gain more subscribers. This can be a win-win situation for both parties involved, as they can tap into each other's audience and gain exposure to new viewers.

Another example of the supportive community on YouTube is the use of hashtags and challenges. By using hashtags and participating in challenges, YouTubers can connect with others in the community and build their brand. This is a fun way to engage with your audience and showcase your creativity, while also making new friends and building relationships with other YouTubers.

The current landscape of the YouTube community is both exciting and challenging, but it's essential to understand the landscape in order to succeed. By embracing the diversity of content, the tight-knit community, and the endless opportunities, you can set your channel apart from the competition and reach your goals.

In conclusion, the YouTube community is a dynamic and ever-changing landscape, but it's also one of the most supportive and exciting platforms for beginner teenage YouTubers. With a little hard work, dedication, and a touch of creativity, you can make your mark on the YouTube community and turn your passion into a successful channel. So, don't be afraid to dive in, embrace the challenges, and unleash your creativity!

Differentiating oneself from the competition

Differentiating oneself from the competition is a crucial step in the journey of becoming a successful YouTuber. With millions of channels and content creators on YouTube, it can be daunting to stand out from the crowd and make a name for oneself. However, this challenge is not insurmountable. By embracing your unique qualities, finding your niche, and creating authentic content, you can differentiate yourself from the competition and build a strong, loyal audience.

The first step in differentiating oneself from the competition is to embrace your unique qualities. You are a one-of-a-kind individual with a unique perspective, interests, and passions. These qualities make you who you are, and they are what set you apart from other content creators. Embracing your individuality and incorporating it into your content is key to standing out from the crowd. For example, if you have a quirky sense of humor, incorporate that into your videos. If you have a passion for cooking, make cooking tutorials that showcase your unique approach. By embracing your individuality, you are sending a clear message to your audience that you are not just another generic content creator – you are someone special, with a unique voice and perspective.

Finding your niche is another important step in differentiating yourself from the competition. YouTube is a vast platform with millions of channels covering a wide range of topics. By focusing on a specific niche, you can hone in on your strengths and create content that appeals to a specific audience. For example, if you love all things beauty, focus on creating beauty tutorials and reviews. If you have a passion for gaming, create gaming content that showcases your skills and insights. By focusing on a specific niche, you are able to differentiate yourself from the competition and attract a dedicated audience.

Another key aspect of differentiating oneself from the competition is creating authentic content. In today's world, audiences are looking for content that feels real, genuine, and authentic. They want to connect with content creators who are true to themselves and who are not afraid to show their true colors. By creating content that is authentic and true to yourself, you are sending a message to your audience that you are not just putting on a show – you are a real person with real passions and interests. For example, if you are passionate about environmental issues, create videos that showcase your knowledge and advocacy efforts. If you have a strong sense of humor, create videos that showcase your funny side and make your audience laugh.

One of the biggest advantages of being a YouTuber is the ability to connect with your audience on a personal level. By creating content that is authentic, engaging, and entertaining, you can build a strong, loyal audience who will stick with you through thick and thin. Whether it's through live streams, Q&A sessions, or other interactive content, connecting with your audience will help you differentiate yourself from the competition and build a strong, dedicated following.

In conclusion, differentiating oneself from the competition is a crucial step in the journey of becoming a successful YouTuber. By embracing your unique qualities, finding your niche, and creating authentic content, you can stand out from the crowd and build a strong, dedicated audience. Whether it's through live streams, Q&A sessions, or other interactive content, connecting with your audience will help you differentiate yourself from the competition and build a strong, dedicated following. Remember, the key to success is to be true to yourself and to create content that is authentic, engaging, and entertaining. So go ahead, embrace your individuality and make your mark on YouTube!

Utilizing competition as motivation and learning opportunities

As a beginner teenage YouTuber, competition can be intimidating and overwhelming. With so many talented individuals in the YouTube community, it's easy to feel like you're fighting an uphill battle. However, competition can also be a powerful source of motivation and learning. By embracing the competition, you can harness its energy to drive you towards success.

First and foremost, competition can be a great motivator. When you see other YouTubers creating amazing content and growing their channels, it can inspire you to work harder and be more creative. You may find yourself driven to produce better content and put your all into your channel. This increased effort can result in significant improvements in your content quality and help you grow your channel.

In addition to motivation, competition can also provide valuable learning opportunities. By observing the success of others, you can learn what works and what doesn't. You can see what kind of content your audience is drawn to and what they enjoy watching. This information can be incredibly useful in developing your own content strategy. Furthermore, you can learn from the mistakes and missteps of others, avoiding common pitfalls and focusing your energy in the right direction.

It's important to remember that competition should be approached with a healthy and positive attitude. Rather than viewing other YouTubers as threats, see them as partners in growth. When you view competition in this way, it becomes an opportunity to collaborate, network and build relationships with other creators in the community. This can lead to exciting opportunities to work on projects together, cross-promote each other's channels and offer support and encouragement to one another.

So how do you use competition as motivation and a learning opportunity? The key is to approach it with an open mind and a willingness to learn. Take the time to study other YouTubers in your niche, watch their videos and pay attention to what makes them successful. Look for ways you can differentiate your channel from theirs, but also don't be afraid to try new things based on their successes. When you encounter a challenge or setback, don't give up. Instead, use the experience as an opportunity to learn and grow.

One example of a YouTuber who utilized competition as motivation and a learning opportunity is Jenna Marbles. She began her channel in 2010 and was competing against many established comedians and content creators. Rather than being intimidated by the competition, she embraced it and used it to drive her own growth. She worked hard to differentiate herself, honing her unique brand of humor and creating relatable content that resonated with her audience. As a result, she built a massive following and became one of the most successful female YouTubers of all time.

Another example is Casey Neistat, who started his channel in 2010. He was initially intimidated by the abundance of talented filmmakers on YouTube, but he didn't let that stop him. Instead, he used the competition as a motivator, constantly pushing himself to create better and more engaging content. Over time, his dedication paid off and he built a massive following and became a leading figure in the YouTube community.

In conclusion, competition can be a powerful source of motivation and learning for beginner teenage YouTubers. By embracing the competition, you can harness its energy to drive you towards success. Use it to motivate yourself to create better content, and as a learning opportunity to see what works and what doesn't. Remember to approach competition with a positive attitude, viewing other YouTubers as partners in growth. With the right mindset and a willingness to learn, competition can be a valuable tool in your journey to success as a YouTuber.

Chapter 5

Time Management

Time management is a crucial aspect of life, especially for teenage YouTubers who have a lot on their plate. Balancing school, hobbies, relationships, and content creation can be a daunting task, leaving many feeling overwhelmed and stressed. But with effective time management, you can achieve your goals, prioritize your well-being, and avoid burnout.

Time management is all about being intentional with your time and making the most of each moment. It requires discipline and effort, but the rewards are endless. By taking control of your time, you can reduce stress, increase productivity, and achieve a better work-life balance.

Imagine waking up every morning with a clear schedule and a sense of purpose. You feel organized and in control, knowing exactly what needs to be done and when. You're able to attend all your classes, spend quality time with friends and family, and still have time to create amazing content for your channel. Sounds like a dream come true, right? Well, with time management, it can be a reality.

The first step in effective time management is setting goals. This means determining what you want to achieve and creating a plan to get there. This could be anything from finishing a project, reaching a certain number of subscribers, or simply having more free time. Once you've set your goals, you can then create a schedule that prioritizes the tasks necessary to reach those goals.

It's also important to be realistic with your schedule and avoid overloading yourself with too many tasks. This is where the concept of "less is more" comes into play. By focusing on a few key tasks each day, you'll be able to achieve more in less time. For example, instead of trying to create a video every day, aim for two videos a week, but make sure they're high-quality and engaging. This way, you'll have more time for other things and be able to put your best foot forward in your content creation.

One of the biggest challenges of time management is sticking to the schedule. It's easy to get sidetracked or become overwhelmed, but with discipline and perseverance, you can stay on track. One helpful tool is a daily to-do list, which allows you to track your progress and hold yourself accountable. You can also use an app or planner to help keep you organized and on track.

Another important aspect of time management is avoiding procrastination. This means taking action on your tasks instead of putting them off until later. By avoiding procrastination, you'll be able to get more done in less time and reduce the stress and anxiety that come with it. To avoid procrastination, try breaking down tasks into smaller, manageable chunks and setting a deadline for each. This will help you avoid feeling overwhelmed and keep you motivated to get things done.

Finally, it's important to prioritize self-care in your time management. This means taking breaks when you need them, engaging in physical activity, and spending time with loved ones. When you take care of yourself, you'll be able to perform at your best and achieve your goals. It's also important to remember that it's okay to say "no" to things that don't align with your priorities. By being mindful of your time and energy, you'll be able to avoid burnout and lead a more fulfilling life.

In conclusion, time management is a vital skill for teenage YouTubers and anyone looking to achieve their goals and live a balanced life. By setting goals, creating a schedule, avoiding procrastination, and prioritizing self-care, you'll be able to take control of your time and succeed in your journey. So start taking action today, and see how effective time management can transform your life.

Examples of time management strategies that teenage YouTubers can use include:

Wake up early and start the day with a positive mindset. This gives you a head start on the day and allows you to be productive from the get-go.

Set aside dedicated time for content creation and stick to it. This means no distractions, no procrastination, just pure focus on creating amazing content.

Use a timer to stay on track and avoid getting sidetracked. This will help you stay focused and avoid wasting time on irrelevant tasks.

Plan your week in advance and prioritize your tasks based on their importance. This allows you to be more productive and avoid feeling overwhelmed.

Take regular breaks to avoid burnout and refresh your mind. This can be as simple as going for a walk, meditating, or spending time with loved ones.

Learn to say "no" to things that don't align with your priorities. This means avoiding distractions and staying focused on your goals.

Use technology to your advantage. Apps like Trello, Google Calendar, and Todoist can help you stay organized and manage your time effectively.

Time management is a life-long journey, but with dedication and effort, anyone can become a master. By adopting these strategies, you'll be able to achieve your goals, reduce stress, and lead a fulfilling life as a teenage YouTuber. So take action today and start making the most of your time.

Balancing YouTube content creation with other responsibilities

Balancing YouTube content creation with other responsibilities is a challenging task for many beginner teenage YouTubers. With the desire to grow their channel and produce high-quality content, it can be difficult to manage the demands of everyday life, such as school, work, friends, and family. The pressure to keep up with the demands of content creation can be overwhelming and can cause stress and burnout. However, it is possible to find a balance and make YouTube content creation a positive and enjoyable experience.

As a beginner, it is essential to understand the importance of prioritizing and managing your time effectively. Content creation requires a significant amount of time and energy, but it shouldn't consume all of your time and prevent you from participating in other activities that bring joy and fulfillment to your life. It's important to strike a balance between content creation and other responsibilities, such as school and work.

One way to balance your time is to set realistic goals for yourself. Instead of setting a goal to produce a video every day, consider setting a goal to produce one or two videos per week. This will give you more time to focus on other responsibilities and prevent burnout. Additionally, it's essential to take breaks and give yourself time to recharge. Allocating time to your other interests and hobbies can help prevent burnout and provide you with new inspiration for your videos.

Another way to balance your time is to make use of technology. With the availability of scheduling and productivity apps, it's possible to keep track of your tasks and appointments in one place. You can use these tools to schedule your content creation time and ensure that you are staying on track. Additionally, these tools can also help you stay organized and prioritize your tasks, making it easier to manage your time effectively.

It's also important to communicate your content creation goals and schedule with your friends and family. Letting them know the time and effort you put into creating videos will help them understand why you need to balance your time and responsibilities. Having their support and understanding can help reduce stress and make it easier to balance your time.

For example, consider a beginner YouTuber named Sarah who is also a full-time college student. She wants to grow her channel but struggles to find the time to create videos and keep up with her studies. To balance her time, Sarah sets a goal to produce one video per week and schedules her content creation time on weekends. She also uses a productivity app to keep track of her schedule and ensure that she stays on track. With the support of her friends and family, Sarah is able to balance her time effectively and produce high-quality content that her followers love.

In conclusion, balancing YouTube content creation with other responsibilities is a challenging but achievable task for beginner teenage YouTubers. By setting realistic goals, utilizing technology, communicating with friends and family, and taking breaks, it's possible to strike a balance and make content creation a positive and enjoyable experience.

Remember, content creation should not consume all of your time and prevent you from participating in other activities that bring joy and fulfillment to your life. Finding a balance will not only help you grow your channel but also bring happiness and balance to your life.

Creating a schedule and sticking to it

Creating a schedule and sticking to it is a crucial step for beginner teenage YouTubers to achieve success. A well-structured schedule can help you balance your YouTube content creation with other responsibilities, save time, increase productivity, and achieve your goals. In this section, we will discuss how to create a schedule and the benefits of sticking to it.

Creating a schedule is a straightforward process that starts with defining your goals. What do you want to achieve with your YouTube channel? Do you want to create new content every day? Or once a week? Determine your goals and then break them down into smaller, achievable tasks. For example, if your goal is to create a new video every week, break it down into tasks such as researching ideas, filming, editing, and uploading.

Once you have your tasks defined, prioritize them and allocate time for each. Consider the time required for each task and the importance of each in achieving your goal. Then, organize your schedule around your other commitments, such as school or work. Remember to leave time for breaks and leisure activities, as well. A well-balanced schedule will help you avoid burnout and keep you motivated.

Sticking to your schedule is just as important as creating one. A schedule is only as good as its ability to keep you on track. Consistency is key in building and growing your YouTube channel. Set yourself up for success by following your schedule rigorously. If you find yourself struggling to stick to your schedule, consider setting reminders or enlisting the help of a friend or family member.

One of the benefits of sticking to a schedule is increased productivity. When you have a plan in place, you'll be able to get more done in less time. You'll avoid the distractions that come with trying to create content on the fly. You'll also be able to prioritize the most important tasks and focus on them without wasting time on less critical tasks.

Another benefit of sticking to a schedule is increased motivation. When you have a plan in place, it's easier to stay focused and driven towards your goals. You'll feel more in control of your time and less stressed, knowing that you have a plan in place. You'll also be able to measure your progress more effectively and feel a sense of accomplishment as you achieve your goals.

For example, let's say that you have a goal of creating a new video every week. You have allocated four hours on Monday to research and brainstorm ideas, two hours on Tuesday to film, three hours on Wednesday to edit, and one hour on Thursday to upload and promote your video. By sticking to this schedule, you'll have a new video every week and you'll feel a sense of accomplishment knowing that you've met your goal.

In conclusion, creating a schedule and sticking to it is essential for beginner teenage YouTubers. It allows you to balance your YouTube content creation with other responsibilities, increase productivity, and achieve your goals. By setting a plan in place and sticking to it, you'll feel more in control, motivated, and focused on your YouTube journey. So, take the time to create a schedule and stick to it. Your channel and your mental health will thank you for it.

Delegating tasks and finding ways to maximize efficiency

Delegating tasks and finding ways to maximize efficiency is a critical aspect of being a successful teenage YouTuber. It can be overwhelming to balance the creation of high-quality content with the numerous other responsibilities that come with being a teenager. Whether it's school, sports, or social activities, it can feel like there just aren't enough hours in the day. However, with the right approach to delegating tasks and maximizing efficiency, it is possible to achieve a healthy balance and create the content you love.

The first step to delegating tasks is to identify what tasks can be delegated to others. It's essential to determine which tasks are essential for you to handle and which tasks can be handled by someone else. For example, you may want to delegate tasks such as editing, research, or administrative tasks to someone who is more experienced or has more free time. By delegating these tasks, you free up time to focus on the tasks that require your unique skills and creativity.

Once you've identified the tasks that can be delegated, it's time to find the right people to delegate them to. It's crucial to choose people who you trust and who have the skills and experience to handle the tasks effectively. You may consider hiring a virtual assistant or seeking out the help of friends or family members who have the skills and experience to assist you. You can also look for online communities or forums where you can find help and connect with other YouTubers who are looking for help with similar tasks.

Once you have found the right people to delegate tasks to, it's essential to communicate your expectations clearly and provide them with the resources and information they need to complete the tasks successfully. This may include providing them with a detailed list of instructions, access to your content management system, or access to your social media accounts.

In addition to delegating tasks, finding ways to maximize efficiency is crucial to staying productive and organized. One effective way to maximize efficiency is to create a schedule and stick to it. This can help you stay focused and avoid wasting time on tasks that aren't essential. By creating a schedule, you can prioritize your tasks and ensure that you have enough time to complete everything.

Another way to maximize efficiency is to make use of technology and tools. There are many tools and apps available that can help you stay organized, manage your time, and automate tasks. For example, you can use a project management tool like Trello to keep track of your tasks, set deadlines, and collaborate with others. You can also use a time tracking app to monitor how much time you spend on each task and identify areas where you can improve.

It's also essential to take breaks and take care of yourself to maximize efficiency. When you're feeling burned out, it can be challenging to stay productive and focused. Taking breaks to recharge and do something you enjoy can help you come back to your tasks with renewed energy and a clear mind. This can also help you avoid burnout and maintain your motivation to create content.

In conclusion, delegating tasks and finding ways to maximize efficiency are critical components of being a successful teenage YouTuber. By delegating tasks to others, you can free up time to focus on the tasks that require your unique skills and creativity. By maximizing efficiency through creating a schedule, making use of technology and tools, and taking breaks, you can stay organized and productive, and achieve a healthy balance in your life.

Here's an example to illustrate this point:

Imagine you are a teenage YouTuber who has just started your channel and is already feeling overwhelmed with the amount of work that needs to be done. You have to create content, edit videos, promote your channel, and manage your social media accounts, all while balancing school, sports, and your social life. You feel like you are constantly running out of time and can't keep up with everything.

One day, you decide to take a step back and assess the situation. You realize that you can delegate some of your tasks, such as editing and research, to others who have more experience and free time. You also realize that you can maximize your efficiency by creating a schedule and sticking to it, making use of technology and tools, and taking breaks to recharge.

You start by reaching out to a friend who is experienced in video editing, and you offer to pay them for their services. Your friend agrees, and you provide them with a detailed list of instructions and access to your content management system. This frees up a significant amount of your time, and you can now focus on creating content and promoting your channel.

Next, you use a project management tool like Trello to keep track of your tasks and set deadlines. You also use a time tracking app to monitor how much time you spend on each task, and you identify areas where you can improve. You find that you are much more organized and productive, and you are able to complete your tasks in a timely manner.

Finally, you make sure to take breaks and take care of yourself. You realize that taking breaks and doing something you enjoy can help you come back to your tasks with renewed energy and a clear mind. This helps you avoid burnout and maintain your motivation to create content.

In the end, you are able to balance your responsibilities and create high-quality content for your channel. You feel proud of yourself for taking the steps necessary to delegate tasks and maximize your efficiency, and you are now able to enjoy the process of creating content for your YouTube channel.

By delegating tasks and maximizing efficiency, you can achieve a healthy balance in your life and be successful as a teenage YouTuber. Don't let the overwhelming feeling of too much work hold you back from creating the content you love. Take control, delegate tasks, and maximize your efficiency, and you'll be on your way to success.

Chapter 6

Social Media Pressure

Social media pressure is a real and palpable thing that affects many teenage YouTubers. It can be overwhelming, stressful and at times even debilitating. The constant need to be popular, to have more followers and to be seen as successful can take its toll on a young person's self-esteem and mental health. In this section, we will delve deeper into the social media pressure that beginners face and offer some coping mechanisms to help them navigate it.

The pressure to be popular is omnipresent on social media platforms. It seems like everyone else is doing better, and the constant comparison can be soul-crushing. Teenagers are naturally vulnerable and still figuring out who they are, and the pressure to be seen as popular and successful can be especially hard for them to bear. The constant need to be perfect, to have the latest gadgets, the best clothes and the most followers can be exhausting. It's like a never-ending cycle of needing to keep up with the Joneses and it's exhausting.

It's not just about being popular though, it's about being accepted. Social media has created a virtual world where people are judged on their online presence, and for many teenagers, this can be their entire world. If they don't have enough followers, if their content isn't popular, it can feel like they are being rejected. This rejection can be devastating to a young person's self-esteem, especially when they are already navigating the challenges of adolescence.

The pressure to be popular can also lead to unhealthy habits. Teenagers may feel compelled to buy followers or likes to make their channel seem more successful. They may also engage in other behaviors that can have serious consequences, like cyberbullying or spreading false information. It's easy to forget that there is a real person behind every screen and that our actions can have real consequences.

It's not just the pressure to be popular that can be overwhelming, it's also the pressure to be perfect. Every post, every video, every picture has to be just right. The need to be perfect can be debilitating, and it can lead to a lack of creativity and a fear of taking risks. It can also lead to a negative body image and a distorted view of reality.

So what can be done about it? The first step is to recognize that social media pressure is a real thing and that it can have real consequences. It's important to understand that there is no such thing as a perfect life, and that everyone's journey is different. It's also important to remember that social media is not real life. It's a curated version of our lives, and it's not a true representation of who we are or what our lives are like.

It's also important to find healthy ways to cope with the pressure. One way is to limit your exposure to social media. Take a break from it, or limit your use to a certain amount of time per day. It's also important to surround yourself with positive people who support and encourage you. Find a community of like-minded individuals who can support you and help you navigate the challenges of social media.

Another way to cope with social media pressure is to focus on what you're doing, not on what others are doing. Focus on your own journey and your own goals. Don't compare yourself to others and don't let their success or popularity dictate your worth. Find joy in the journey and embrace the challenges that come with it.

Finally, it's important to find your own voice and to be true to yourself. Don't try to be someone you're not. Embrace your unique qualities and let your personality shine through in your content. The more authentic you are, the more likely you are to attract a following of people who appreciate you for who you are. Remember that your channel is not just about having followers, it's about connecting with people and creating meaningful content. When you focus on creating content that you love, your passion and energy will shine through, and that is what will attract an audience.

In conclusion, social media pressure is a real and challenging issue that many teenage YouTubers face. It can be overwhelming, stressful and at times even debilitating. However, it is important to remember that social media is not real life and that there is no such thing as a perfect life. It's also important to find healthy ways to cope with the pressure, like limiting your exposure to social media, surrounding yourself with positive people, focusing on your own journey, finding your own voice, and being true to yourself. When you focus on these things, you will find that social media pressure becomes less and less of an issue, and that you can navigate it with confidence and grace.

Understand the Pressure to be Popular and Gain Followers:

As a beginner teenage YouTuber, it's easy to get caught up in the race to gain followers and become popular on social media. The pressure to be noticed and make a name for yourself in the YouTube community can be overwhelming. Social media can be a cruel and ruthless place, with the constant need for validation and the pressure to present a perfect image. The desire to be popular is not just a teenage problem, but it's a common problem faced by people of all ages in this digital age. However, this pressure can be particularly intense for teenage YouTubers who are just starting out and still trying to find their footing in the world of online content creation.

The impact of this pressure can be severe, affecting one's mental health and self-esteem. The constant comparison to other YouTubers who seem to have more followers, better equipment, and more impressive content can lead to feelings of inadequacy and frustration. It's easy to fall into the trap of thinking that you're not good enough and that you'll never reach your goals. This self-doubt can be debilitating, causing you to lose motivation and give up on your dreams.

However, it's important to remember that success is not defined by the number of followers you have. The truth is that popularity does not equate to happiness or fulfillment. The pressure to be popular is a trap, and it's important to resist the urge to conform to these unrealistic standards. Instead, focus on creating content that you're proud of and that truly represents who you are.

One of the best ways to overcome this pressure is to connect with other YouTubers who are facing the same struggles. Joining online communities, attending events, and participating in collaborations can help you to feel supported and less alone. These connections can also provide you with new perspectives and ideas, and help you to grow as a content creator.

Another way to overcome this pressure is to focus on creating content that you're passionate about. When you're creating content that you truly love, the need for validation from others becomes less important. You'll find that your passion and drive to create will sustain you even when the going gets tough.

For example, if you're passionate about music, focus on creating music-related content that you're passionate about. Don't try to follow the latest trends or what's popular at the moment, but instead, stay true to your passions and interests. If you're truly passionate about what you're doing, your followers will be able to sense it, and your content will naturally attract the right audience.

Another example is if you're passionate about travel, focus on creating travel-related content that you're passionate about. Whether it's exploring new destinations, sharing your travel experiences, or showcasing your favorite travel gear, your passion for travel will shine through in your content. This will help you to build a loyal following who will support and encourage you on your journey.

In conclusion, it's important to understand that the pressure to be popular and gain followers is just a façade. The truth is that success is not defined by the number of followers you have, but by the quality of your content and the impact that it has on your audience. By staying true to your passions and interests, you can overcome the pressure to be popular and create content that truly represents who you are. So, forget about the pressure to be popular and focus on creating content that you're proud of, and your followers will naturally follow.

Developing a Healthy Relationship with Social Media and Avoiding Comparison

As a teenage YouTuber, it can be easy to get caught up in the pressure of social media and the constant need to compare yourself to others. The need to gain followers, likes, and comments can lead to a toxic and unhealthy relationship with social media. But it's important to remember that social media is just a tool to connect with others and promote your content, not a reflection of your worth or success.

Social media can often present a distorted reality where people only show their highlight reels. The constant exposure to these carefully curated images and videos can lead to feelings of inadequacy and self-doubt. But it's important to remember that everyone's journey is different and to focus on your own progress and growth, rather than comparing yourself to others.

Comparison can lead to feelings of anger, frustration, and resentment. It can also lead to a lack of motivation and a decline in self-esteem. To avoid comparison, it's important to focus on your own goals and aspirations, rather than comparing yourself to others. Remember that everyone's journey is unique, and what works for others may not work for you.

It's also important to cultivate a positive mindset and surround yourself with positive influences. Seek out supportive and encouraging people in your life, and limit your exposure to negative or toxic individuals. Surround yourself with positivity and encouragement, and focus on the things that bring you joy and fulfillment.

One way to develop a healthy relationship with social media is to set boundaries and limit your exposure. Turn off notifications, limit your screen time, and take breaks from social media when necessary. You can also unfollow or mute accounts that make you feel insecure or inadequate.

Another way to cultivate a healthy relationship with social media is to focus on meaningful and authentic engagement. Engage with your followers and interact with other content creators in a positive and supportive manner. Use social media as a tool to connect with others and promote your content, rather than a source of validation or self-worth

Finally, it's important to find a healthy balance between promoting your content and maintaining your privacy. Protect your personal information and be mindful of the content you share online. Remember that what you post on social media is permanent and can have a lasting impact on your reputation and future opportunities.

In conclusion, developing a healthy relationship with social media and avoiding comparison is essential for your mental and emotional well-being as a teenage YouTuber. Focus on your own goals and progress, surround yourself with positive influences, and set boundaries to limit your exposure to negative or toxic individuals. Cultivate a positive mindset, engage in meaningful and authentic interactions, and balance your promotion of your content with privacy concerns. By following these tips, you can build a strong and successful career as a teenage YouTuber while avoiding the pitfalls of social media comparison and negativity.

Focusing on meaningful and authentic engagement with followers

Focusing on meaningful and authentic engagement with followers is a crucial aspect of building a strong online presence as a teenage YouTuber. With the constant pressure to gain more followers and be popular, it can be easy to lose sight of what truly matters when it comes to engaging with your audience. However, if you want to build a lasting connection with your followers and grow your channel, it's important to focus on meaningful and authentic engagement.

Meaningful engagement involves connecting with your followers in a genuine way, showing them that you value their support and appreciate their presence on your channel. This can be achieved through various means such as responding to comments, asking for feedback, and creating content that resonates with your audience. When you focus on meaningful engagement, you're not only building a strong connection with your followers but also creating a community that supports and encourages you on your journey as a YouTuber.

One way to create meaningful engagement is by responding to comments and messages. Taking the time to reply to comments shows your followers that you value their thoughts and opinions. It's a great way to start a conversation with your audience and get to know them better. By responding to comments and messages, you can create a sense of community and connection that encourages followers to keep coming back to your channel.

Another way to focus on meaningful engagement is by asking for feedback. This can be done through a dedicated Q&A video, an Instagram story poll, or a dedicated email address for feedback. When you ask for feedback, you're showing your followers that you're open to constructive criticism and value their opinions. Feedback can also be a great way to get ideas for new content and understand what your audience wants to see from you.

Creating content that resonates with your audience is another important aspect of meaningful engagement. When you make content that speaks to your followers, you're creating a connection that goes beyond just the number of views and subscribers. This could mean creating content that addresses common questions or concerns, or simply creating content that reflects the values and interests of your audience. When you create content that resonates with your followers, you're creating a bond that encourages them to stay engaged and support your channel.

However, meaningful engagement is only one half of the equation. The other half is authenticity. Authenticity is about being true to yourself and your values, and being honest and transparent with your audience. When you're authentic, you're creating a connection that goes beyond just your content, and into the realm of who you are as a person. Authenticity is what sets you apart from other YouTubers and encourages followers to stick around and support you.

For example, a teenage YouTuber who focuses on mental health might share their own struggles with anxiety or depression in a video. This not only connects with their audience, who may be going through similar struggles, but it also shows their followers that they are genuine and willing to be vulnerable. By being authentic, the YouTuber creates a sense of trust and relatability that encourages followers to keep coming back to their channel.

Another example is a teenage YouTuber who focuses on beauty and fashion. Instead of just creating videos about the latest trends, they might also share their personal style and the meaning behind their fashion choices. This not only sets them apart from other beauty and fashion YouTubers, but it also creates a sense of authenticity and relatability that encourages followers to support their channel.

In conclusion, focusing on meaningful and authentic engagement with followers is a crucial aspect of building a strong online presence as a teenage YouTuber. By connecting with your followers in a genuine way, responding to comments and messages, asking for feedback, creating content that resonates with your audience, and being true to yourself and your values, you're creating a community that supports and encourages you on your journey. By focusing on meaningful and authentic engagement, you're not only building a strong connection with your followers, but you're also creating a bond that goes beyond just views and subscribers. It's this connection that will help you grow your channel and achieve your goals as a YouTuber. So, always remember to focus on meaningful and authentic engagement and never compromise your values or authenticity in order to gain more followers or views. Your audience will appreciate and support you for being yourself, and that is what will ultimately lead to success.

Chapter 7

Privacy Concerns: The Constant Threat to Your Online Safety

As a beginner teenage YouTuber, you are likely eager to share your creative work with the world and engage with your followers. But as you open up your life to the world, you also expose yourself to the dangers of online privacy violations. Privacy concerns can be a major source of anxiety, leaving you feeling vulnerable and exposed. In this digital age, protecting your personal information and online safety is of utmost importance.

Imagine waking up one day to find that someone has hacked into your social media accounts, using your personal information for malicious purposes. Maybe they've changed your profile picture, posted inappropriate content, and spread false rumors about you. The thought of having your personal information and reputation tarnished is a scary one. This is just one of the many examples of how your privacy can be compromised online.

Another example is when your private photos or videos are leaked without your consent. This could ruin your reputation, cause emotional distress, and even impact your future opportunities. You may have shared these photos with someone you trust, only for them to betray that trust and use the information for their own gain. This can lead to feelings of embarrassment, shame, and anger.

Privacy concerns don't just impact your personal life. They can also affect your channel and the success of your content. Imagine having a popular channel with thousands of subscribers, only to have it shut down because of privacy violations. All of your hard work and effort could be gone in an instant, leaving you feeling helpless and defeated.

These are just a few examples of the many ways that privacy concerns can affect your life as a teenage YouTuber. But the good news is that there are steps you can take to protect your privacy and maintain control of your personal information. Here are some tips to help you stay safe online:

Be mindful of what you share online: Before you post anything online, think carefully about the potential consequences. Consider whether the information you're sharing is sensitive or could be used against you in some way.

Keep your passwords secure: Use strong passwords and avoid using the same password for multiple accounts. Enable two-factor authentication whenever possible, and change your passwords regularly.

Be careful with personal information: Be wary of giving out your personal information, such as your full name, address, phone number, and financial information. Consider using a pseudonym or alias to protect your identity.

Watch out for phishing scams: Phishing scams are fraudulent emails or messages that appear to be from a legitimate source but are actually designed to steal your personal information. Always be cautious of emails or messages that ask for sensitive information and only provide personal information through secure websites and services.

Be mindful of the apps and websites you use: Only use apps and websites that have a good reputation and take privacy seriously. Read their privacy policy and terms of service before sharing any information with them.

Be careful with your photos and videos: Be mindful of the photos and videos you share online, as they can be easily shared or leaked. Avoid sharing sensitive or intimate photos and videos and consider using encryption or privacy settings to protect your content.

Stay informed and update your privacy settings: Stay informed about the latest privacy concerns and make sure to regularly review and update your privacy settings on your social media and online accounts.

By taking these precautions and being mindful of your online presence, you can protect your privacy and stay safe online. While privacy concerns can be a major source of anxiety, it's important to remember that you have the power to take control of your personal information and maintain your online safety.

In conclusion, as a beginner teenage YouTuber, it's important to prioritize your privacy and take steps to protect your personal information. From being mindful of what you share online to staying informed about the latest privacy concerns, you can safeguard your online safety and continue to pursue your passion for creating content. So, don't let privacy concerns hold you back. Take control of your online presence and continue to make a positive impact in the world of YouTube.

Balancing privacy with the need to engage with followers

Balancing privacy with the need to engage with followers can be a tricky and delicate dance for beginner teenage YouTubers. On one hand, it's important to maintain control over personal information and protect privacy online. On the other hand, engaging with followers and building a relationship with them is crucial for growth and success on YouTube. Finding the right balance can be challenging, but with the right guidance and mindset, it is achievable.

When it comes to privacy, it is essential to remember that anything posted online can potentially be seen by millions of people, and it's crucial to be mindful of what information is shared. This can range from personal details like home addresses and phone numbers, to more subtle things like emotional reactions and personal opinions. Teenagers are often still figuring out who they are, and the last thing they want is for the whole world to know their secrets or have the wrong impression of them.

It's also important to consider the future. What might seem harmless now could have serious consequences in the future, such as damaging reputation or even limiting job prospects. For example, posting pictures or videos of reckless or inappropriate behavior can have serious consequences, and it's important to be mindful of what is being shared online.

However, engaging with followers and building relationships is also a crucial part of growing a successful channel on YouTube. Responding to comments and messages, sharing personal experiences and opinions, and connecting with followers through live streams are all ways to build a loyal and engaged community. This type of interaction and connection can lead to growth and success on the platform.

So, how can beginners find a balance between maintaining privacy and engaging with followers? Here are a few tips to get started:

Know your boundaries: Before starting a YouTube channel, it's important to have a clear understanding of what information is comfortable to share and what isn't. This can be as simple as creating a list of personal details that are off-limits, or thinking through specific scenarios where privacy might be compromised.

Be selective: When it comes to sharing personal information, it's important to be selective. For example, sharing details about hobbies or interests is a great way to engage with followers without compromising personal privacy.

Use pseudonyms: Using a pseudonym or alias can be a great way to maintain privacy while still engaging with followers. This allows creators to separate their personal and public lives, and it can also make it easier to manage feedback and comments.

Be mindful of reactions: Emotional reactions can be a double-edged sword, as they can be incredibly powerful in building relationships with followers, but they can also reveal too much personal information. It's important to be mindful of how reactions are shared and to think through the potential consequences before hitting "post".

Take control of personal information: Taking control of personal information is crucial for maintaining privacy online. This can include deleting old posts, adjusting privacy settings on social media platforms, and being mindful of what is shared on public forums like YouTube comments.

Ultimately, balancing privacy with the need to engage with followers is about finding what works best for each individual creator. With a clear understanding of personal boundaries, selective sharing, and mindful reactions, beginners can build successful channels on YouTube while maintaining control over personal information.

In conclusion, finding the balance between privacy and engagement is a crucial aspect of building a successful YouTube channel. By understanding the importance of privacy, being mindful of reactions, and taking control of personal information, beginners can find the right balance and grow their channels while maintaining control over their personal lives.

Protecting personal information online

Protecting personal information online is one of the most crucial yet often overlooked aspects of using the internet. With the rise of social media and online platforms, it has become easier than ever to share information about ourselves, but it has also become easier for hackers, scammers, and cyber criminals to access and misuse that information.

Imagine logging onto your bank account one day to find that all your savings have been transferred to an unknown account. Or, receiving an email from someone pretending to be a trusted friend, asking for personal information. These scenarios may seem far-fetched, but they happen all too often in the digital age. Every time we post a photo, tweet a thought, or fill out a survey, we are giving away pieces of ourselves, and it can all add up to a wealth of sensitive information.

But what can we do to protect our privacy online? The first step is to be mindful of the information we are sharing. Limit the personal details you post publicly, such as your full name, home address, or phone number. Be careful about which apps you download and what information you share with them. Avoid clicking on links from unknown sources and never share personal information in response to an unsolicited email.

Another way to protect personal information online is to use strong passwords and change them regularly. Make sure to use a combination of letters, numbers, and symbols, and avoid using the same password for multiple accounts. Enable two-factor authentication wherever possible, as this adds an extra layer of security to your accounts.

It's also important to keep software and security systems up to date. Regularly update your computer's operating system and anti-virus software to ensure that your computer is protected against the latest threats.

Another way to protect personal information online is to be wary of phishing scams. Phishing scams are emails or messages that appear to come from a trustworthy source, such as a bank or an online retailer, but are actually fake. The goal of these scams is to trick you into giving away sensitive information, such as login credentials or credit card numbers. Always be cautious of emails or messages that ask for personal information, and never enter personal information into a website that you reach by clicking a link in an email.

It's also important to be mindful of public Wi-Fi networks. Public Wi-Fi networks are often unsecured, which means that anyone on the same network can see the information you are sending or receiving. Avoid using public Wi-Fi networks for sensitive transactions, such as online banking or shopping. If you must use a public Wi-Fi network, use a virtual private network (VPN) to encrypt your internet connection.

In conclusion, protecting personal information online is a critical aspect of using the internet. By being mindful of what we share, using strong passwords, keeping software up to date, being wary of phishing scams, and being careful when using public Wi-Fi networks, we can help protect ourselves against cyber threats and keep our sensitive information safe. The consequences of not doing so can be devastating, so it's important to take the necessary steps to protect our privacy online.

Understanding the importance of online privacy and security

The internet is a powerful tool that connects us with the world, but with this convenience comes the risk of having our personal information exposed and vulnerable. As a teenager, it is important to understand the importance of online privacy and security to protect ourselves and our future. In a world where social media, online shopping, and digital communication dominate, it is imperative to take control of our online presence and keep our information safe.

Online privacy and security are essential for protecting our personal information from being used against us. Whether it is our name, address, phone number, credit card information, or other sensitive data, this information can be used by cyber criminals for malicious purposes such as identity theft, hacking, and online fraud. Imagine having your entire life savings wiped out because someone managed to steal your bank information. Imagine having your reputation tarnished because someone used your name and picture to spread false information online. These are not just far-fetched scenarios, they are real possibilities that can happen to anyone who does not take their online privacy and security seriously.

Moreover, privacy and security are also crucial for protecting our personal relationships and emotional well-being. Social media platforms have become a significant part of our lives, connecting us with friends and family, and giving us the opportunity to express ourselves. However, these platforms can also be used to spread negativity, bullying, and harassment. If our personal information is not secure, it can be used to hurt us or those we care about. It is imperative to protect ourselves and our loved ones by taking steps to secure our online presence.

So, how can we protect our online privacy and security? The first step is to be aware of the types of information we share online. Be cautious about what you post on social media and be mindful of the privacy settings on your accounts. Avoid sharing sensitive information, such as financial information or passwords, and never click on suspicious links or download attachments from unknown sources.

Another way to protect your privacy and security is to use strong and unique passwords for all your accounts. Make sure your passwords are at least 12 characters long and include a combination of numbers, letters, and symbols. It is also recommended to change your passwords regularly to prevent unauthorized access.

Another important step is to use antivirus software and firewalls to protect your computer and mobile devices from cyber attacks. Keep your software updated and be vigilant when downloading files and apps.

It is also essential to be cautious about the websites you visit and the information you provide. Before entering any sensitive information, make sure the website is secure by checking for a padlock icon in the address bar or "https" in the URL. Be wary of phishing scams that aim to steal your information, and never provide your personal information to untrusted sources.

Finally, it is important to educate yourself and others about online privacy and security. Teach your friends and family about the importance of keeping their information safe and the steps they can take to protect themselves. Spread awareness about the dangers of online fraud and cybercrime, and encourage others to take action to secure their online presence.

In conclusion, online privacy and security are crucial for protecting our personal information, relationships, and emotional well-being. It is our responsibility to take control of our online presence and make sure our information is secure. By being mindful of what we share, using strong passwords, and protecting our devices, we can keep our information safe and secure. Don't wait until it's too late – start taking action today to protect your online privacy and security.

Chapter 8

Feedback: The Ultimate Test of Resilience

As a beginner YouTuber, there's nothing more nerve-wracking than waiting for feedback from your viewers. It's like standing in front of a crowd, waiting for the verdict on your performance. You're vulnerable and exposed, and your heart races as you anticipate the judgment. Feedback can either uplift you or tear you down, and it's a crucial part of the YouTube journey that requires resilience.

Receiving feedback can be an emotional rollercoaster. There's a rush of excitement when you receive positive comments, and it feels like a validation of your hard work. But when negative comments come rolling in, it can be crushing. The sting of criticism can feel like a sharp knife to the heart, and it's easy to let it get to you. The truth is, feedback is not personal, but it's human nature to take it that way.

However, feedback is an opportunity to grow and improve, and it's essential to take it in stride. As a beginner YouTuber, feedback can be intimidating, but it's an opportunity to learn and make your channel better. It's a chance to see your content from a different perspective and make changes that can bring your channel to new heights.

One of the key things to remember about feedback is that it's subjective. Everyone has different opinions and preferences, and what may be a positive comment to one person may be negative to another. So, it's important to take feedback with a grain of salt and not let it define you.

For example, if you receive a comment that says your content is boring, it's important to consider the source and the context. Is it coming from someone who is not your target audience? Or is it coming from someone who has high standards and is looking for something more advanced? It's important to not let one negative comment discourage you, but instead, use it as a learning opportunity. Ask yourself what you can do differently to make your content more engaging and appealing to your viewers.

When it comes to feedback, it's essential to have a growth mindset. A growth mindset is the belief that you can improve and grow through effort and learning. It's about embracing challenges and viewing feedback as a learning opportunity. A growth mindset allows you to take feedback in stride and not let it define you.

For example, if you receive a comment that says your editing is poor, it's essential to have a growth mindset and view it as a challenge. You can take the opportunity to improve your editing skills and make your content better. You can learn new techniques, invest in editing software, and practice until you're confident in your skills.

Finally, it's important to remember that feedback isa two-way street. While it's essential to receive feedback from your viewers, it's also important to give feedback to others. As a beginner YouTuber, you can learn a lot from other creators, and giving feedback can help you build relationships and connect with others in the community. When giving feedback, it's essential to be constructive and offer suggestions that can help improve the channel.

For example, if you come across a channel that you admire, you can offer feedback by commenting on the things that you enjoy about their content and offering suggestions for areas that could be improved. This will not only help the creator, but it will also help you develop a better understanding of what makes great content.

In conclusion, feedback is a crucial part of the YouTube journey, and it's essential to embrace it with a growth mindset. Whether you're receiving or giving feedback, it's a learning opportunity that can help you improve and grow your channel. Remember, feedback is not personal, and it's essential to take it with a grain of salt and view it as an opportunity to grow. With resilience and a growth mindset, you can turn feedback into a valuable tool that can take your channel to new heights.

Understanding the Different Types of Feedback

Feedback is an essential part of the growth process for any beginner YouTuber. It helps you understand what works and what doesn't, and gives you the opportunity to improve your content and reach a wider audience. However, feedback can be a double-edged sword and it's important to understand the different types of feedback you may receive, and how to handle them in a healthy and constructive way.

Positive Feedback

Positive feedback is the type of feedback that can boost your confidence and give you the motivation to keep creating. This type of feedback usually comes in the form of compliments, praise, or words of encouragement. For example, "I really loved your latest video, it was so entertaining and informative!" or "I'm so impressed with your editing skills, keep up the great work!" Positive feedback is a great way to feel appreciated and recognized for your efforts. It's important to acknowledge and embrace this type of feedback, and let it fuel your passion for creating content.

Constructive Feedback

Constructive feedback is the type of feedback that is meant to help you improve your content. It's not always easy to hear, but it's important to take it in stride and use it to your advantage. This type of feedback usually comes in the form of suggestions, criticism, or advice. For example, "Your audio quality could use some improvement,consider investing in a better microphone," or "Maybe try to add more variety to your content by trying different formats like Q&A or reaction videos." Constructive feedback can be tough to receive, but it's a valuable tool that can help you grow and improve as a YouTuber. It's important to listen with an open mind, ask clarifying questions, and try to see things from the perspective of the person giving the feedback. You may not always agree with the feedback, but it's important to consider it, and take the necessary steps to improve your content.

Negative Feedback

Negative feedback can be the toughest type of feedback to handle, especially when it comes in the form of harsh criticism or insults. This type of feedback can range from a simple disagreement to full-blown online attacks. For example, "Your content is boring and unoriginal, you need to do better," or "You're a terrible YouTuber and I can't believe anyone watches you." It's important to remember that negative feedback is not a reflection of who you are as a person, but rather a reflection of the opinion of the person giving the feedback. In most cases, it's best to ignore negative feedback and avoid engaging in online drama.

General Feedback

General feedback is the type of feedback that is a mix of positive, constructive, and negative feedback. This type of feedback usually provides a well-rounded view of your content and can give you a better understanding of what's working and what's not. For example, "Your intro was really catchy, but I think you need to work on the lighting in your videos." This type of feedback is a great starting point for improving your content and reaching a wider audience.

In conclusion, feedback is an important tool for growth, and it's important to understand the different types of feedback you may receive. Positive feedback can boost your confidence and motivation, constructive feedback can help you improve your content, negative feedback is best ignored, and general feedback provides a well-rounded view of your content. Remember to listen with an open mind, ask clarifying questions, and use feedback to your advantage. And most importantly, never let feedback get in the way of your passion for creating content and pursuing your dreams.

Accepting feedback as constructive criticism and using it to improve

Accepting feedback as constructive criticism is a crucial aspect of growth for beginner teenage YouTubers. Feedback can be hard to hear, but it's an opportunity to improve your content and build a better relationship with your followers. With the right attitude and approach, feedback can become an invaluable tool for success on YouTube.

As a beginner, it can be tempting to get discouraged by negative feedback. It's important to understand that negative feedback is not a reflection of your worth as a person or a YouTuber. Instead, it's an opportunity to learn, grow, and get better. Remember, the ultimate goal is to create content that your followers love and appreciate. Feedback is a way to get closer to that goal.

It can be hard to keep a level head when receiving negative feedback, especially when it's delivered in an unkind or hurtful way. But, it's important to remember that negative feedback is not personal. You are not your channel, and your channel is not you. Try to approach feedback objectively and understand that the goal is to improve your content, not to take it personally.

One of the best ways to approach feedback is to view it as a gift. Your followers are taking the time to provide you with their thoughts and opinions on your content. This is a valuable opportunity to learn what your followers like and what they would like to see more of. Feedback can help you identify areas that need improvement, so you can make changes that will positively impact your channel and your followers.

To make the most of feedback, it's important to be open-minded and listen actively. Take the time to read each comment and consider the perspective of the person providing the feedback. Try to understand the reasoning behind their thoughts and opinions, and look for patterns in the feedback. This can help you identify areas that need improvement and make changes that will have a lasting impact on your channel.

It's also important to avoid taking feedback too seriously. Remember that everyone has different opinions, and not all feedback will be relevant or applicable to your channel. Focus on the feedback that is most helpful and relevant, and don't be afraid to ask for clarification or additional information if you need it.

Another key aspect of accepting feedback is to respond thoughtfully and respectfully. Acknowledge the feedback and thank your followers for taking the time to provide it. If you disagree with the feedback, explain why and provide your perspective. And, if you agree with the feedback, let your followers know that you appreciate their input and are making changes to improve your content.

Here are a few examples of how to use feedback as constructive criticism to improve your channel:

Improving the quality of your videos: If you're receiving feedback that your videos are shaky or blurry, consider investing in a tripod or stabilizer. If the audio quality is poor, look into upgrading your microphone or taking steps to improve the acoustics of your filming location. These small changes can make a big difference in the quality of your videos and help you stand out from the competition.

Experimenting with new content: If your followers are requesting new types of content, consider experimenting with different topics and formats. You may discover a new passion or niche that you never considered before. And, your followers will appreciate the effort you're making to provide them with new and exciting content.

Building a stronger connection with your followers: If you're receiving feedback that your videos feel impersonal or detached, consider incorporating more of your personality into your content. Share stories and experiences that are relevant to your channel and connect with your followers on a deeper level. This willhelp you build a stronger community and create a more engaging and personalized experience for your followers.

Improving your time management: If you're receiving feedback that your videos are inconsistent or take too long to upload, consider refining your time management skills. Make a schedule and stick to it, prioritize your tasks, and find ways to streamline your workflow. This will help you maintain a consistent upload schedule and improve the quality of your videos.

Addressing privacy concerns: If you're receiving feedback about privacy concerns, it's important to take steps to protect your personal information and the privacy of those around you. This can include blurring faces or backgrounds, avoiding sharing sensitive information, and being mindful of the content you're sharing.

In conclusion, accepting feedback as constructive criticism is essential for growth as a beginner teenage YouTuber. It's important to approach feedback objectively, listen actively, and respond thoughtfully. By using feedback to improve your content, you can create a better experience for your followers, build a stronger community, and ultimately achieve success on YouTube.

Dealing with negative feedback and avoiding online drama

Dealing with negative feedback and avoiding online drama can be one of the biggest challenges for beginner teenage YouTubers. The online world is a double-edged sword - it gives you a platform to showcase your talent, but it also exposes you to criticism and drama. The pressure to be perfect and maintain a good image can be overwhelming, but it's essential to remember that negative feedback is not personal. In this chapter, we'll explore how to deal with negative feedback and avoid online drama.

First and foremost, it's important to understand that not everyone will like what you do, and that's okay. In the online world, people are more likely to leave negative comments, and it's crucial to keep this in mind when dealing with feedback. Negative feedback can be hurtful, and it's normal to feel upset when someone criticizes your work. However, it's important to take a step back and look at the situation objectively. Most of the time, negative feedback is not a reflection of your talent or your worth as a person.

When dealing with negative feedback, it's crucial to remain calm and composed. Don't react impulsively and avoid getting defensive. Instead, take the time to think about the feedback and determine if there's anything you can learn from it. If the feedback is constructive, use it to improve your content. If it's not helpful or if it's rude, ignore it.

It's also important to remember that online drama is often fueled by anonymous comments and keyboard warriors. People who hide behind anonymity often say things they wouldn't say in person. Don't give them the satisfaction of engaging in a back-and-forth argument. Avoid online drama at all costs, and if you do find yourself in a situation where someone is being rude or aggressive, the best thing to do is to block them.

One of the best ways to avoid online drama is to maintain a positive attitude. Stay focused on your goals, and don't let negative feedback or drama derail your progress. Surround yourself with supportive people who believe in you and your work.

Seek out other YouTubers and form a community where you can share your experiences and offer each other support.

Finally, it's crucial to take care of yourself. Creating content can be a time-consuming and emotionally draining process, and it's essential to prioritize self-care. Take breaks when you need them, and don't be afraid to reach out for help if you're feeling overwhelmed. Remember that your mental health and well-being should always come first.

In conclusion, dealing with negative feedback and avoiding online drama is a crucial aspect of being a teenage YouTuber. Negative comments can be hurtful, but it's important to keep in mind that they're not personal. Remain calm, use constructive feedback to improve your content, avoid online drama, maintain a positive attitude, and prioritize self-care. With these tips, you can overcome the challenges and enjoy the journey of creating content on YouTube.

Example:

Let's imagine you're a teenage YouTuber who creates makeup tutorials. You've just uploaded a new video, and you've received a negative comment that says, "Your makeup looks terrible, you should stick to cooking." The comment is hurtful, and you feel upset and frustrated.

Here's what you can do to deal with this situation:

Take a step back and don't react impulsively. Don't engage in a back-and-forth argument with the commenter.

Evaluate the feedback. Is there anything you can learn from it? In this case, the comment is not helpful or constructive.

Ignore the comment and focus on the positive feedback. Most of your followers love your tutorials and appreciate your work. Remember that negative comments are not representative of your entire audience.

Take care of yourself. Make sure to prioritize self-care and don't let the negative comment affect your mental health.

Surround yourself with supportive people who believe in you and your work. Reach out to other

YouTubers and form a community where you can share your experiences and offer each other support.

Maintain a positive attitude. Stay focused on your goals and don't let negative feedback or drama derail your progress.

By following these tips, you can overcome the challenges of dealing with negative feedback and avoid online drama. Remember that as a beginner YouTuber, you're bound to face criticism and drama, but with a positive attitude and self-care, you can overcome these challenges and continue to create amazing content.

Chapter 9

Growing the Channel

Growing a YouTube channel can be a thrilling yet challenging journey, especially for beginner teenage YouTubers. The thrill of having your own platform to share your passions, reach a wider audience and make a difference in the world, is a dream come true for many. But, with the ever-growing competition, it can be easy to feel overwhelmed and discouraged. However, with the right mindset and strategies, growing your channel can be an exciting and rewarding experience.

The key to growing your channel is consistency and persistence. YouTube algorithms favor channels that consistently upload high-quality content on a regular schedule. This not only helps your audience stay engaged and anticipate new content, but it also helps your channel rank higher in the search results, making it easier for new viewers to discover your channel.

It is essential to find a schedule that works for you and stick to it. Whether it is once a week or twice a day, finding a routine that you can realistically maintain will make all the difference in the growth of your channel. Make sure to upload content that is fresh, unique, and relevant to your audience. Utilize social media platforms like Twitter, Instagram, and Facebook to promote your content and reach a larger audience. Building a strong online presence will not only help you reach more people but also create a loyal and engaged following that will support you as you grow.

Networking with other YouTubers can also be a valuable tool in growing your channel. Collaborating with others in your niche can bring new viewers to your channel and open up opportunities for future collaborations. Engage with other YouTubers by commenting, liking and sharing their content. The more you engage with others, the more likely they are to return the favor and share your content with their audience. Building relationships in the YouTube community will not only help you grow your channel, but it will also create meaningful connections and opportunities for future collaborations.

Finding your niche and differentiating yourself from the competition is essential to growing your channel. Whether it's through your unique perspective, humor, or personality, make sure your channel stands out from the rest. Embrace your individuality and let it shine through in your content. Your audience will appreciate your authenticity and reward you with their loyalty and support.

Implementing growth strategies such as creating eye-catching thumbnails, optimizing your video titles, and adding keywords to your video descriptions will help you reach a wider audience. Utilize search engine optimization (SEO) techniques to improve your videos' search ranking and increase visibility. Partner with brands and sponsors to monetize your channel and reach an even larger audience. With the right strategies and tools, the possibilities for growth are endless.

One of the most important things to remember when growing your channel is to stay true to yourself and your passions. While it can be tempting to chase after the latest trends and try to be like everyone else, it is crucial to remember that your unique voice and perspective is what sets you apart and makes you special. Don't be afraid to take risks and try new things. Your audience will appreciate your authenticity and support you in your creative journey.

In conclusion, growing a YouTube channel can be a challenging but rewarding journey. With consistency, persistence, and the right strategies, you can reach new heights and make a difference in the world through your passions and creativity. Remember to stay true to yourself, embrace your individuality, and never give up on your dreams. The journey may be long, but the rewards are endless.

Example:

Imagine a teenage YouTuber who has been creating beauty and fashion content for six months. Despite her consistent posting schedule and high-quality content, she feels discouraged by the lack of growth in her channel. She begins to question her niche and feels overwhelmed by the competition. But, she decides to take a step back and reassess her strategies. She begins to network with other beauty and fashion YouTubers, collaborate on videos and promote each other's content. She also starts to incorporate her unique personality and humor into her videos, making her content stand out from the rest. By taking these steps and never giving up on her passion, she begins to see growth in her channel and a more engaged audience. She continues to monetize her channel through partnerships with brands and sponsors and never forgets the importance of staying true to herself and her passions. Her channel becomes a huge success and she becomes a role model for other beginner teenage YouTubers, inspiring them to never give up on their dreams and to always stay true to themselves.

Understanding the importance of consistency and persistence

Consistency and persistence are the backbone of success in any field, and YouTube is no exception. For beginner teenage YouTubers, these two traits can make all the difference between a channel that fizzles out after a few months and one that grows and flourishes. Understanding the importance of consistency and persistence is crucial for anyone who wants to achieve their goals on the platform.

Consistency is all about maintaining a regular and steady pace. It's about sticking to a schedule and uploading videos on a regular basis. When viewers know when they can expect new content from you, they are more likely to tune in and become loyal followers. By being consistent, you're telling your viewers that you value their time and that you're dedicated to providing them with high-quality content. This is the foundation of building a strong and engaged audience.

Persistence, on the other hand, is about never giving up. It's about pushing through the tough times and continuing to work towards your goals, even when the road ahead seems impossible. As a beginner, there will be times when you face challenges and obstacles. It's natural to feel discouraged and frustrated, but persistence is what will help you overcome these obstacles and continue on your journey. When you're persistent, you're sending a message to yourself and your audience that you're in this for the long haul. You're not just a flash in the pan. You're a dedicated content creator with a vision and a plan.

The combination of consistency and persistence is powerful. When you're consistent in your content creation and persistent in your efforts, you're sending a message of commitment and dedication. Your audience will pick up on this and they will be more likely to support you and follow you on your journey. In turn, this will give you the confidence and motivation you need to keep pushing forward, even when the going gets tough.

Let's take a look at some examples of how consistency and persistence can help you grow your channel.

First, let's consider the story of a YouTuber who has a passion for beauty and makeup. She starts out by posting videos once a week, but after a few months, she gets busy with school and other responsibilities. As a result, she stops posting videos for several weeks. When she finally gets back to posting, her viewers have lost interest and her channel has lost momentum. This is a perfect example of how consistency is crucial for maintaining a strong and engaged audience.

Now, let's look at another example of a YouTuber who loves to play video games. He starts out by posting videos every other day, but after a few months, he loses motivation. He starts to feel like he's not making progress and that no one is watching his videos. However, he decides to persist and continue posting videos, even though it's difficult. Over time, he starts to see results. His viewers begin to engage more with his content, and he starts to gain new followers. This is a perfect example of how persistence can pay off in the long run.

Finally, let's consider a YouTuber who is passionate about cooking. She starts out posting videos once a week, but she also adds in a few daily vlogs to give her viewers a more in-depth look at her life. Over time, her viewers start to connect with her on a personal level and they become more invested in her channel. As a result, she starts to gain more followers and her channel grows. This is a perfect example of how combining consistency and persistence can help you grow your channel and build a strong relationship with your audience.

In conclusion, consistency and persistence are the keys to success on YouTube. As a beginner, it can be easy to get discouraged and lose motivation, but by keeping a steady pace and never giving up, you can achieve your goals and grow your channel. Whether you're facing a lack of content ideas, competition, time management issues, social media pressure, privacy concerns, feedback, or just trying to grow your channel, consistency and persistence will always be there to help you push through the tough times.

Remember, the journey to success is never easy, but with consistency and persistence, anything is possible.

Utilizing social media platforms and networking to reach a larger audience

Utilizing social media platforms and networking to reach a larger audience is an essential part of growing a successful YouTube channel. In today's digital age, social media has become the hub of communication, where people from all over the world come together to connect, share, and express themselves. As a beginner teenage YouTuber, it is important to understand the power of social media and how to harness it to reach a larger audience.

The first step in utilizing social media platforms is to have a strong presence on them. This means having a complete and well-crafted profile, sharing engaging and relevant content, and interacting with your followers. By doing so, you can build a loyal following that will support and promote your channel. Furthermore, by consistently posting quality content and engaging with your followers, you can establish yourself as a trusted and credible source of information.

In addition to having a strong presence on social media platforms, networking is also crucial for reaching a larger audience. This means connecting and collaborating with other YouTubers and content creators in your niche. Not only will this help you expand your reach, but it can also lead to meaningful and long-lasting relationships that can benefit you in many ways. For example, by collaborating with another YouTuber, you can reach their audience and gain new subscribers, while they can do the same for you. Furthermore, by working together, you can create high-quality content that will engage and inspire your audiences.

Networking with other YouTubers and content creators doesn't have to be complicated or time-consuming. There are many online communities and groups dedicated to helping YouTubers connect and collaborate with each other. For example, by joining a Facebook group or a subreddit dedicated to your niche, you can meet and connect with other like-minded individuals who share your passion and interests. Additionally, attending events and conferences that are relevant to your niche can also be a great way to network and connect with others in the industry.

Another way to utilize social media platforms and networking to reach a larger audience is by creating and promoting content that is shareable. This means creating content that is visually appealing, entertaining, and relevant to your target audience. By doing so, you will inspire your followers to share your content with their friends and followers, thereby expanding your reach and increasing your visibility. For example, if you create a viral video that is both entertaining and educational, it can easily be shared on social media platforms and reach a much larger audience.

In conclusion, utilizing social media platforms and networking is a crucial step in growing your YouTube channel and reaching a larger audience. By building a strong presence on social media platforms, connecting with other YouTubers and content creators, and creating shareable content, you can establish yourself as a credible and trusted source of information and inspiration. Remember, success on YouTube doesn't happen overnight, but by utilizing social media platforms and networking, you can increase your visibility, reach more people, and achieve your goals as a teenage YouTuber.

Implementing growth strategies and finding what works best for their channel

Growing a channel on YouTube can be a challenging and overwhelming experience, especially for beginner teenage YouTubers. However, with the right strategies in place, you can overcome obstacles and achieve your goals. In this chapter, we will explore the various growth strategies that you can implement to reach a wider audience and build a successful channel.

The first step towards growing your channel is to identify your target audience. Who are you making videos for? What kind of content do they enjoy? What are their interests? Once you have a clear understanding of your target audience, you can create content that speaks directly to them and engage with them in a meaningful way.

Social media is a powerful tool for growing your channel. Utilize platforms like Instagram, Twitter, and TikTok to promote your videos and reach a larger audience. Share sneak peeks, teasers, and behind-the-scenes content to give your followers a glimpse into the creative process. Encourage them to share your videos with their friends and followers, and don't be afraid to reach out to other YouTubers and collaborate on content. The more eyes you can get on your channel, the better!

Consistency is key when it comes to growing your channel. It's important to set a schedule for uploading videos and stick to it as much as possible. This not only helps to keep your followers engaged and interested in your content, but it also helps you build a strong brand and establish yourself as a reliable source of content. Aim to upload videos at least once a week, if not more.

Another important aspect of growing your channel is to engage with your audience. Respond to comments, ask for feedback, and build relationships with your followers. This not only helps to foster a sense of community on your channel but it also helps you understand what your audience wants and needs. You can then tailor your content to better meet their needs and keep them coming back for more.

One of the most effective ways to grow your channel is to optimize your videos for search engines. This means using keywords in your video titles, descriptions, and tags that will help your videos show up in search results. Additionally, make sure to include a call-to-action at the end of your videos, encouraging your viewers to like, comment, and subscribe. The more engagement your videos receive, the higher they will rank in search results, increasing your visibility and reach.

Lastly, never stop learning and experimenting with new strategies. You can try new things, like live-streaming, hosting Q&A sessions, or creating a series of videos, to see what works best for your channel. Take the time to analyze your metrics and see which strategies are driving the most engagement and growth. Don't be afraid to make changes and pivot your approach if you're not seeing the results you want.

In conclusion, growing your channel on YouTube can be a rewarding and exciting experience, but it also requires hard work and dedication. By implementing these strategies and finding what works best for your channel, you can reach a wider audience, build a strong brand, and achieve your goals. The journey may not be easy, but the reward of a successful channel is worth every ounce of effort.

So take a deep breath, hold on tight, and let's embark on this exciting journey together! With a little bit of creativity, persistence, and determination, you can turn your passion for YouTube into a thriving channel that resonates with your audience and leaves a lasting impact.

Chapter 10

Conclusion

Becoming a successful teenage YouTuber can be a challenging journey, but it is not impossible. In this book, we have explored the major problems that beginner teenage YouTubers face, from lack of content ideas to privacy concerns, and provided tips and advice on how to overcome them. Throughout this journey, we have emphasized the importance of persistence, creativity, and self-care.

In conclusion, let us reflect on the journey that you have taken thus far. You have read about the struggles and challenges that you may face, and you have learned practical tips and techniques to overcome them. You have learned the importance of having a strong content strategy, using resources to the fullest extent, embracing competition, managing time effectively, navigating social media pressure, protecting privacy, accepting feedback, and growing your channel.

It is time to take what you have learned and put it into action. The road ahead may not be easy, but you have the tools and the knowledge to overcome any obstacle that may come your way. The journey of becoming a successful teenage YouTuber is not just about creating videos, it is about finding your passion and pursuing it with all your heart and soul.

Remember, success is not defined by the number of subscribers you have, but by the impact that your videos have on others. Do not let the pressures of social media or the opinions of others define your success. Instead, focus on creating content that is authentic and meaningful to you. Your uniqueness is what sets you apart from the rest and will attract the right audience to your channel.

The journey to success is not a one-time event, but a continuous process of learning and growth. Do not be afraid to take risks and try new things. Embrace the fear of failure, and use it as fuel to push yourself further. When things get tough, remember why you started this journey in the first place, and let that drive you forward.

Finally, take care of yourself. The journey to success can be draining and stressful, but it is important to prioritize self-care. Set aside time for yourself and engage in activities that bring you joy and peace of mind. Surround yourself with supportive friends and family, and never hesitate to seek help when needed.

In conclusion, becoming a successful teenage YouTuber is not just about creating videos, but about pursuing your passion and growing as an individual. With persistence, creativity, and self-care, you have the power to overcome any obstacle that may come your way. So go forth, create, and make an impact on the world. The journey ahead may be challenging, but the reward of success is worth it.

Example:

Imagine the thrill of hearing that first 'ping' when someone subscribes to your channel, the excitement of receiving positive feedback on your videos, and the joy of watching your channel grow. These are just a few of the many rewards that await you on your journey to becoming a successful teenage YouTuber.

Think about the impact that your videos can have on others, the lives that you can touch and the stories that you can share. Your videos can bring a smile to someone's face on a bad day, offer hope and encouragement to someone who needs it, and create a community of support for those who are struggling.

As you embark on this journey, keep these rewards in mind, and let them motivate and inspire you. Every step that you take, every video that you create, is a step closer to realizing your dream. With persistence, creativity, and self-care, you have the power to overcome any obstacle that may come your way and to achieve success on your own terms.

Recap of the book's main points

In this book, we explored the various challenges faced by beginner teenage YouTubers and offered practical tips and advice to overcome them. Whether it be lack of content ideas, limited resources, competition, time management, social media pressure, privacy concerns, feedback, or growing the channel, each topic was addressed in detail to help beginners navigate the complex world of YouTube content creation.

Lack of content ideas is a common obstacle faced by beginner YouTubers. This challenge can be especially daunting, especially when you're just starting out and trying to establish a presence on the platform. However, we emphasized that with a little creativity and resourcefulness, anyone can overcome this challenge. We encouraged beginners to brainstorm fresh and unique ideas, find inspiration from other YouTubers and non-related sources, and embrace their individuality. By following these tips, beginners will be able to develop a strong content strategy and provide their followers with engaging and captivating content.

Another common challenge faced by beginner YouTubers is a lack of resources. This includes budget constraints and limited access to equipment and editing software. However, we showed that with a little ingenuity and creativity, anyone can create high-quality content with limited resources. We offered practical tips for utilizing available resources to the fullest extent, finding low-cost alternatives, and maximizing efficiency. By following these tips, beginners will be able to overcome their limitations and produce content that is both professional and engaging.

Competition is an inescapable part of the YouTube community. It can be overwhelming for beginners, especially when there are so many other talented individuals vying for the same audience. However, we emphasized that competition can also be a valuable learning opportunity and a source of motivation. We encouraged beginners to differentiate themselves from the competition, embrace their uniqueness, and use competition as a tool to improve their own channel. By following these tips, beginners will be able to thrive in the competitive world of YouTube content creation.

Time management is a critical component of any successful YouTube channel. Balancing content creation with other responsibilities can be difficult, especially for beginners who are just starting out. We offered practical tips for creating a schedule and sticking to it, delegating tasks, and maximizing efficiency. By following these tips, beginners will be able to effectively manage their time and stay organized and productive.

Social media pressure is an all-too-real challenge faced by beginner YouTubers. The pressure to be popular and gain followers can be overwhelming, especially when you're just starting out. We emphasized the importance of developing a healthy relationship with social media and avoiding comparison. We encouraged beginners to focus on meaningful and authentic engagement with their followers, rather than just trying to be popular. By following these tips, beginners will be able to navigate the pressures of social media and build a strong online presence.

Privacy concerns are an increasingly important issue in the digital age. Balancing privacy with the need to engage with followers can be difficult, especially for teenage YouTubers who may not fully understand the risks and consequences of sharing personal information online. We emphasized the importance of online privacy and security, and provided practical tips for protecting personal information online. By following these tips, beginners will be able to protect their privacy while still engaging with their followers.

Feedback is a crucial component of any successful YouTube channel. Whether it's positive or negative, feedback provides valuable insights into how your content is being received by your audience. We emphasized the importance of accepting feedback as constructive criticism and using it to improve. We also offered tips for dealing with negative feedback and avoiding online drama. By following these tips, beginners will be able to effectively navigate the feedback process and use it to grow their channel.

Growing the channel is the ultimate goal of any YouTuber. However, growing a channel can be a slow and difficult process, especially for beginners. We emphasized the importance of consistency, patience, and perseverance. We also offered practical tips for engaging with followers, promoting the channel, and expanding your audience. By following these tips, beginners will be able to grow their channel and reach a larger audience over time.

In conclusion, the world of YouTube content creation can be complex and challenging, especially for beginner teenage YouTubers. However, by facing these challenges head-on and utilizing the tips and advice offered in this book, anyone can overcome the obstacles and build a successful channel. Whether it be lack of content ideas, limited resources, competition, time management, social media pressure, privacy concerns, feedback, or growing the channel, each challenge can be met with determination, creativity, and perseverance. So, embrace your individuality, follow your passion, and let the world see what you have to offer.

Final Thoughts and Encouragement for Beginners

Congratulations! You have taken the first step in embarking on a journey to become a successful teenage YouTuber. The road ahead will be filled with challenges and obstacles, but it is also a path that will bring you immense joy, fulfillment, and opportunities. As you conclude your reading of this book, it is important to take a moment to reflect on the journey so far and look ahead with renewed determination and hope.

The journey to becoming a successful YouTuber can be an emotional rollercoaster, but it is crucial to remember why you started in the first place. You have a unique voice, a unique perspective, and a unique vision for your channel. No one else can bring the same level of passion and excitement to your content as you do. When you feel overwhelmed or discouraged, remind yourself of your passion and purpose. This is what sets you apart and makes you truly special.

You have already taken the first step in overcoming the lack of content ideas by finding inspiration and developing a strong content strategy. Keep in mind that there will be times when you feel creatively blocked, but don't let that discourage you. Take a break, try something new, and don't be afraid to experiment. Some of your best content may come from unexpected sources of inspiration.

The lack of resources can be a significant challenge, but it is also an opportunity to get creative. Use what you have, find low-cost alternatives, and be resourceful. Your audience will appreciate the authenticity and creativity that comes from making the most of limited resources.

Competition can be a source of motivation and learning opportunities. Embrace it, learn from it, and make it work for you. Remember, there is room for everyone on YouTube, and your unique voice and perspective are what set you apart.

Time management is a critical aspect of being a successful YouTuber. Set a schedule, delegate tasks, and prioritize your time. Remember, you are only one person, and it is essential to take care of yourself first.

Don't forget to make time for other important aspects of your life, such as school, friends, and family.

Social media pressure can be overwhelming, but it is important to have a healthy relationship with it. Avoid comparisons, focus on meaningful and authentic engagement, and remember that social media is just a tool to help you grow your channel. Your followers will appreciate your authenticity and genuine engagement more than any superficial online persona.

Privacy concerns are a real issue for teenage YouTubers. Make sure to protect your personal information and be mindful of the content you share online. Remember, once something is posted online, it can never be fully deleted.

Feedback, both positive and negative, is a critical aspect of growing your channel. Use it as a tool to improve and avoid taking negative feedback personally. Remember, not everyone will like your content, and that's okay. The important thing is to stay true to your vision and purpose.

Growing your channel takes time and persistence. Stay consistent, utilize social media platforms, and implement growth strategies. Remember, success is not a destination; it is a journey. There will be ups and downs, but the important thing is to keep moving forward.

In conclusion, becoming a successful teenage YouTuber is a journey filled with challenges and obstacles, but it is also a path that brings immense joy and fulfillment. Remember why you started, embrace the challenges, and never give up on your dream. You are not alone, and there is a supportive community of fellow YouTubers who are eager to help you succeed. So, take a deep breath, hold your head high, and keep pushing forward. You've got this!

www.ingramcontent.com/pod-product-compliance
Lightning Source LLC
Chambersburg PA
CBHW071135220526
45467CB00015B/1100